GW00320470

Sheikh Zayed bin Sultan Al-Nahayyan

President of the United Arab Emirates

Desert life-chain. (Vine).

HERITAGE OF THE UAE

Peter Vine · Paula Casey

Design and illustration by Henry Sharpe

Jacket design by Jane Stark

Front cover photograph by Shirley Kay

Additional Contributors: Linda Coupland
Reem El-Mutwalli
Sarah Searight

Additional Photographers: F. Dipper
H. Eller
C. Furley
C. Gross
M. Hill
S. Kay
T. Larson
J. Usher-Smith
R. Western
T. Woodward

Printed in Japan by Dai Nippon Printing Co.

ISBN 0-907151-39-6

IMMEL PUBLISHING Ltd.
Ely House
37 Dover Street
London W1X 3RB

Tel. 01 491 1799 Fax 01 409 1525
Telex 298582 ELTOUP

Other IMMEL Books by Peter Vine include:

Pearls in Arabian Waters: The Heritage of Bahrain

Jewels of the Kingdom: The Heritage of Jordan

The Heritage of Qatar

The Heritage of Kuwait

Seychelles

The Red Sea

Red Sea Invertebrates

Red Sea Safety Guide

Red Sea Explorers

New Guide to Bahrain

CONTENTS

Introduction	12
The Past	23
Natural History	41
Traditions	81
Art and Artists	116
Modern Emirates	137
Further Reading	158
Acknowledgements	159
Index	160

Dramatic folds of Hajar mountains above Bithna fort. (Kay)

FOREWORD

Those who have lived all their lives in the United Arab Emirates take a special pride in the country's impressive modern strides and its achievements across a broad range of fields, from social to industrial development. Geographically the UAE is immensely varied, from rugged mountainous regions to low mangrove-fringed coastline and from the vast arid desert of the Empty Quarter to fertile oases packed with date-palms and other fruit trees. In recent years the UAE has learnt how to optimise utilisation of its natural resources, developing agriculture and using modern technology to cultivate attractive parks. Its greatest resource, of course is its people, and no effort has been spared in providing the most up to date housing, medical and educational facilities together with highly skilled medics and teachers.

In the past visitors came to explore for oil and minerals, to work in the development and service sectors, or to trade. While these aspects continue to draw people, today their ranks have been added to by genuine tourists who choose to come here for winter sunshine, relaxation and a chance to discover Arabia for themselves.

In this lavishly illustrated new book the authors expertly portray the UAE's historical, cultural, and natural attractions and provide food for thought for both visitors to, and residents of, the United Arab Emirates.

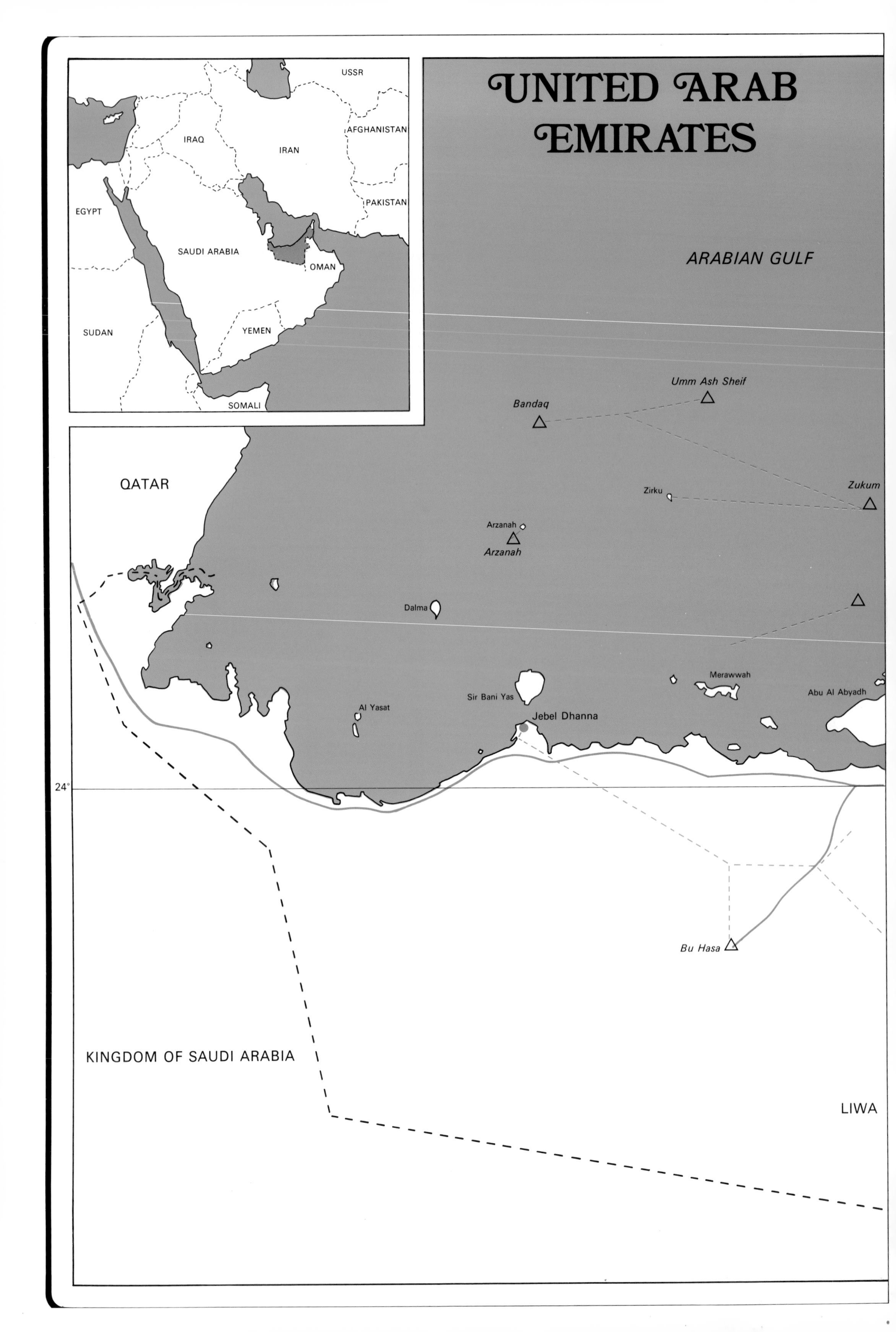
UNITED ARAB EMIRATES
USSR
IRAQ
IRAN
AFGHANISTAN
PAKISTAN
EGYPT
SAUDI ARABIA
OMAN
SUDAN
YEMEN
SOMALI
ARABIAN GULF
Umm Ash Sheif
Bandaq
QATAR
Zirku
Zukum
Arzanah
Arzanah
Dalma
Merawwah
Abu Al Abyadh
Sir Bani Yas
Al Yasat
Jebel Dhanna
24°
Bu Hasa
KINGDOM OF SAUDI ARABIA
LIWA

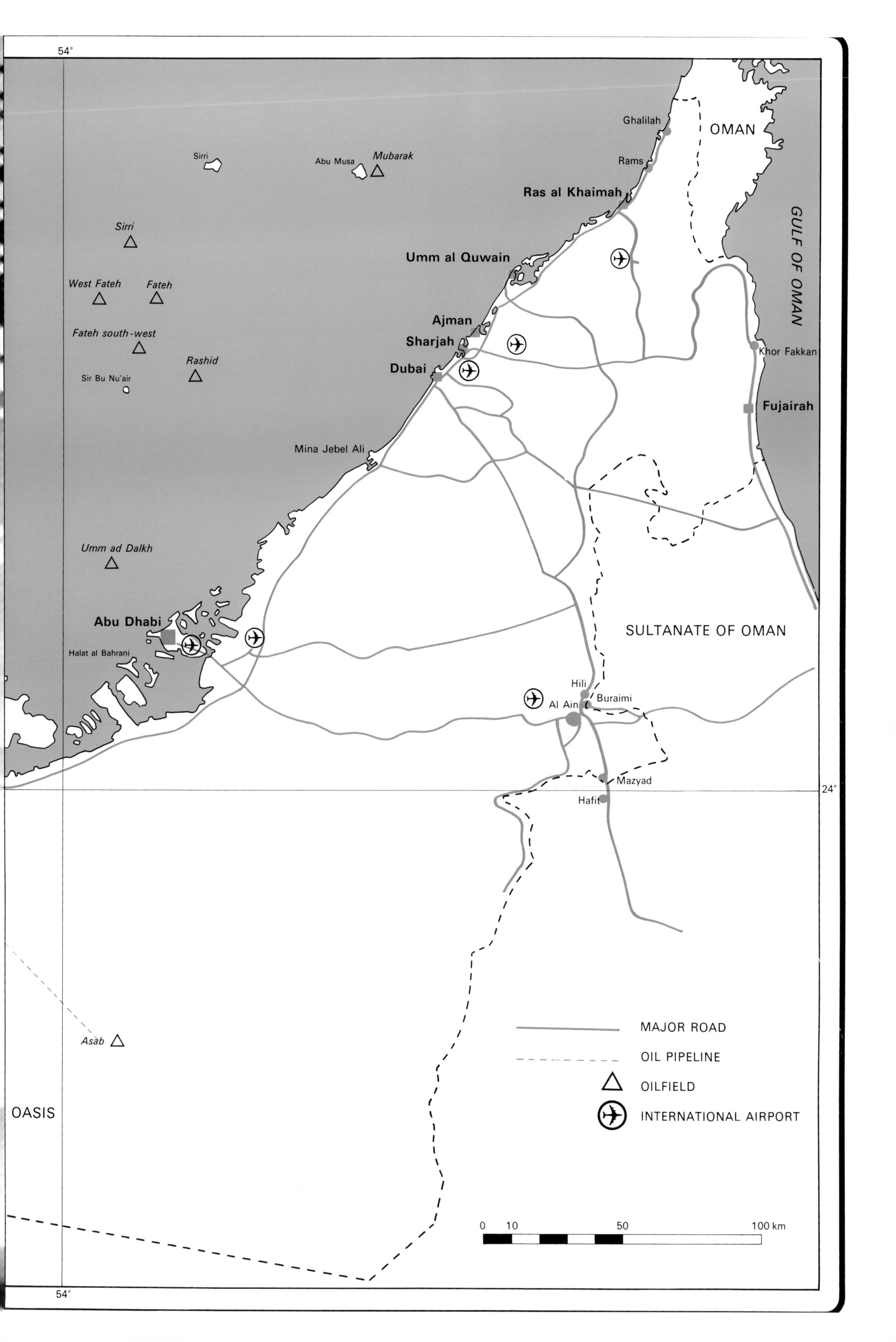

54°
Ghalilah
OMAN
Sirri
Abu Musa
Mubarak
Rams
Ras al Khaimah
GULF OF OMAN
Sirri
Umm al Quwain
West Fateh
Fateh
Ajman
Fateh south-west
Sharjah
Khor Fakkan
Rashid
Dubai
Sir Bu Nu'air
Fujairah
Mina Jebel Ali
Umm ad Dalkh
Abu Dhabi
SULTANATE OF OMAN
Halat al Bahrani
Hili
Buraimi
Al Ain
Mazyad
24°
Hafit
MAJOR ROAD
Asab
OIL PIPELINE
OILFIELD
OASIS
INTERNATIONAL AIRPORT
0
10
50
100 km
54°

INTRODUCTION

Prior to their independence and federalisation in December 1971, the United Arab Emirates was known as the Trucial States, a loosely defined affiliation of the main seven emirates of the peninsula. Earlier it was designated the 'Pirate Coast', an appellation rightly challenged by Dr. Sultan al Qasimi in his recent book, The Myth of Arab Piracy in the Gulf. Much earlier, around 5,000 years ago, the land we now know as the UAE was part of Magan, bordering on the Bitter Sea (Arabian Gulf) along with the neighbouring civilisation of Dilmun (Bahrain). Earlier still, the region was inhabited by Stone Age Man, whose beautifully fashioned flint tools have been found scattered along the foot of the Hajar mountain range. During this period, perhaps eight thousand years ago, a less arid region supported a diverse wildlife upon which Man depended for food. Hundreds of stone tumuli, scattered along the foothills of Jebel Hafit near Al Ain, dating from the end of the 4th millennium BC, provide one of the first indications of an organised settled culture, who buried their dead with some ceremony and whose grave items indicate, at the very least, trading links with Mesopotamia.

This seminal discovery was made by Danish archaeologists commencing the first archaeological investigation in the UAE in 1959, fresh from their excavations of the ancient civilisation of Dilmun in Bahrain. Ancient tombs and settlements from the 3rd millenium on the island of Umm an Nar, near Abu Dhabi, provided them with enough clues to extrapolate that this area corresponded with ancient Magan, the mysterious land referred to on Sumerian clay tablets as a rich source of much-needed raw materials, especially copper. Detailed chemical analysis and research has now proved without any doubt that the copper of the Hajar mountains, present also in residues of castings and crucibles in Umm an Nar sites, was indeed the copper of Magan referred to in the Sumerian cuneiform texts and found in artefacts in Mesopotamia. Work since then has produced a fascinating insight into the country's prehistoric past: these early discoveries at Umm an Nar and Hili, near Al Ain, have been augmented by investigations of newly explored ancient sites throughout the Emirates, indicating a rather widespread early settlement of the region. Much of this interesting

Collection of flint arrowheads dating from the 4th or 5th millennium BC (Kay)

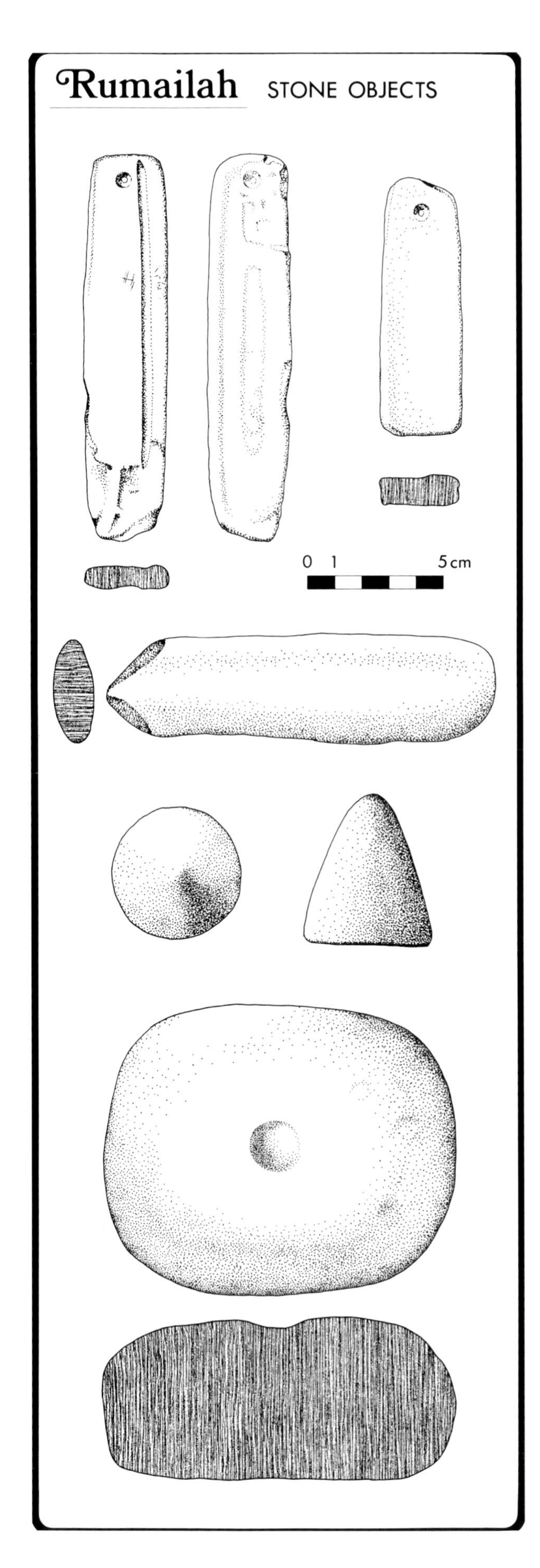

A fine red pot painted with black decoration, from Umm an Nar, is shown at Al Ain Museum. (Kay)

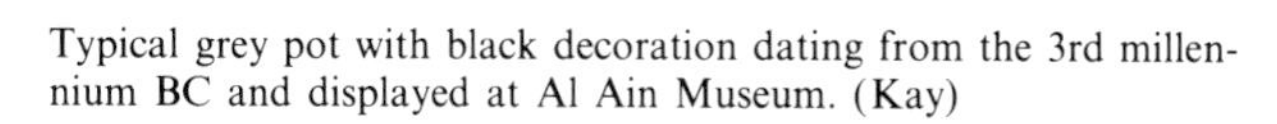

Typical grey pot with black decoration dating from the 3rd millennium BC and displayed at Al Ain Museum. (Kay)

story has been recently told in Shirley Kay's excellent book, Emirates Archaeological Heritage, and is reviewed in greater detail in a series of reports issued by the Department of Antiquities and Tourism, Al Ain, together with a number of scientific journals.

The present picture draws upon archaeological discoveries of recent years, stretching from the identification of the sophisticated Umm an Nar civilisation, which is marked also by some very impressive sites at Hili including a recently reconstructed tomb carved with lions, gazelle and people, as well as seasonal settlements at Ghanada island and tombs at Ajman. As Shirley Kay remarks, to the people of Umm an Nar, copper was as important as is oil to the present inhabitants. To their trading partners in Mesopotamia this vital source of raw metal, timber, limestone and pearls was simply called 'Magan'. But, early in the 2nd millenium, for a number of reasons, all mention of Magan disappears from the written record. A decrease in demand for the area's most important resource brought about by the discovery of iron which was to eventually oust copper from its vital role as the major component in the manufacture of bronze tools and weapons, and a general decline in fortunes suffered by traditional trading partners, were probably the most significant factors affecting Magan's prosperity. It is possible too that a shift to a more arid climate, accompanied by the encroachment of desert sands, rendered living conditions rather arduous in southern Arabia, forcing the inhabitants into a more nomadic lifestyle.

Until recently it appeared that there was a complete gap in the archaeological record at this point, with virtually no evidence of Man's presence during the 2nd millennium BC. This was all changed however by the excavation of a long, narrow sub-surface tomb at Qattara in the Al Ain oasis in which a variety of funerary objects were found, including some beautiful gold dress ornaments, forcing the archaeologists to conclude that

One of two entrance doors to Hili garden tomb, with fine relief carvings. The tomb is believed to date from approximately 2300 BC. (Kay)

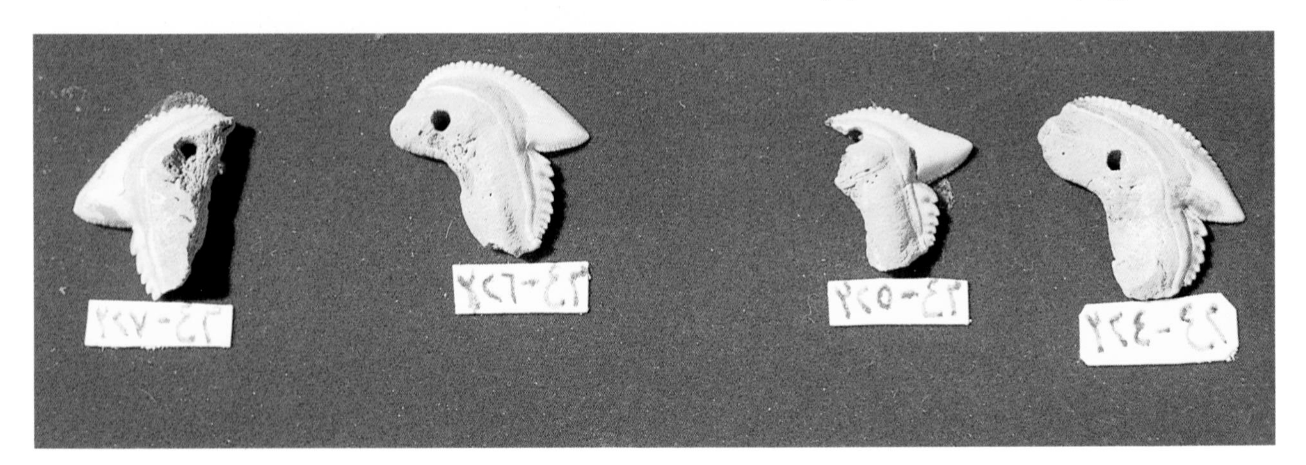

Shark's tooth amulets from Umm an Nar dating from the 3rd millennium BC are displayed at Al Ain Museum. (Kay)

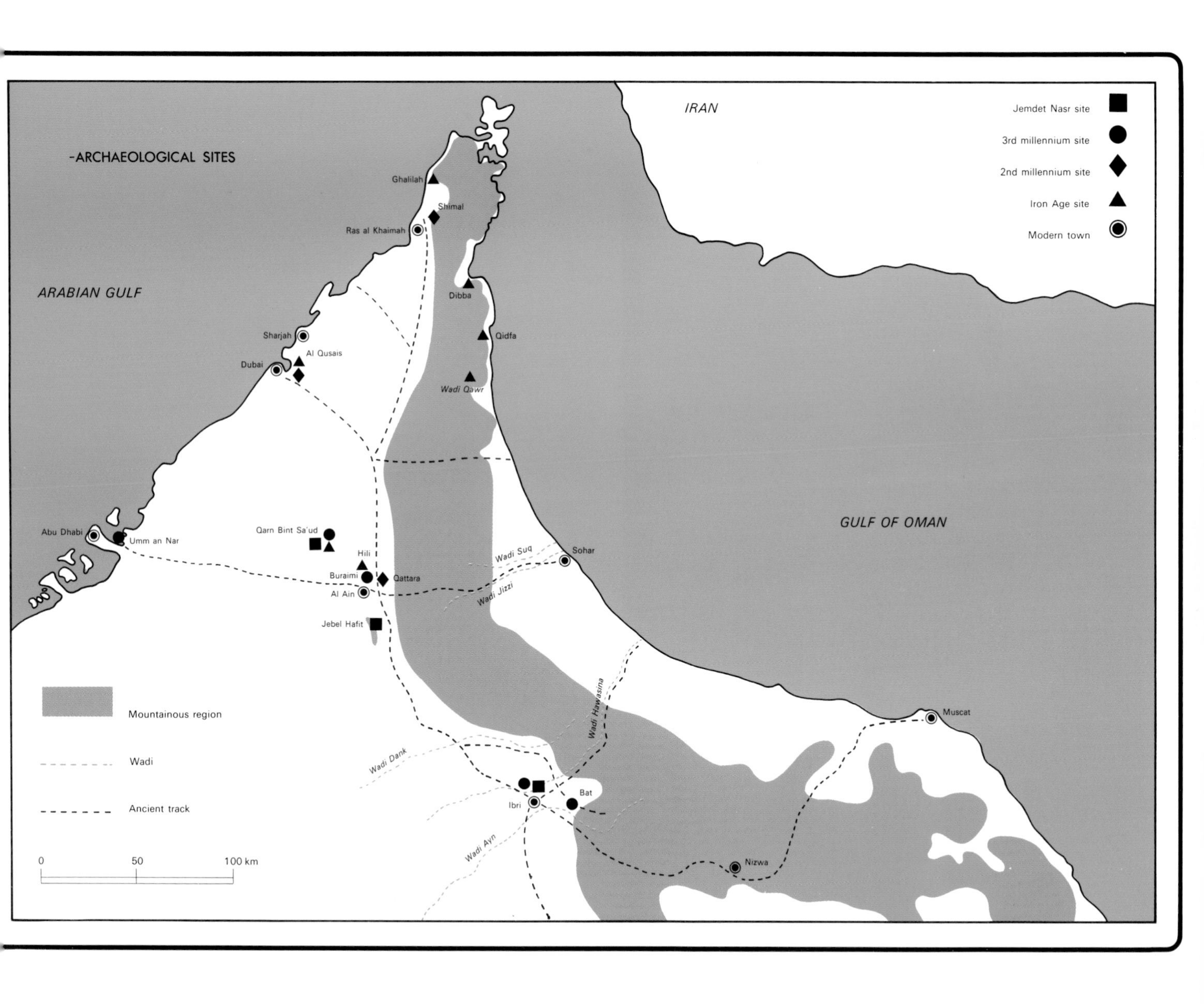

-ARCHAEOLOGICAL SITES
IRAN
ARABIAN GULF
GULF OF OMAN
Jemdet Nasr site
3rd millennium site
2nd millennium site
Iron Age site
Modern town
Ghalilah
Shimal
Ras al Khaimah
Dibba
Qidfa
Wadi Qawr
Sharjah
Al Qusais
Dubai
Abu Dhabi
Umm an Nar
Qarn Bint Sa'ud
Hili
Buraimi
Qattara
Al Ain
Jebel Hafit
Sohar
Wadi Suq
Wadi Jizzi
Wadi Hawasina
Muscat
Wadi Dank
Ibri
Bat
Wadi Ayn
Nizwa
Mountainous region
Wadi
Ancient track
0
50
100 km

2nd millennium BC gold pendant from Qattara tomb, Al Ain (Al Ain Museum). (Kay)

fruits and palm-trees, already grown in the area during the 3rd millenium, was the economic basis of the Al Ain oasis. Other important excavations covering this period are those of Al Qasais, near Dubai; at Wadi Qawr in the Hajar range; and at the village of Qidfa on the east coast. The latter, comprising a grave which was accidentally discovered by a bulldozer driver, yielded a rich hoard of artefacts including bronze bowls, arrowheads, daggers, jewellery, pottery and chlorite containers.

One of the most important towns in the lower Gulf in the Hellenistic period was the port of Ad Dour in Umm Al Quwain where an ancient settlement site now extends across more than two kilometres of desert. Ad Dour's prosperity was clearly linked to its position on important trading routes, potsherds of Roman, Persian and Nabataean origin as well as some coins have been discovered here, but it has so far proved impossible to identify this major city from Roman records. Flourishing also in the late 1st millennium as a result of international trading links was the inland city of Mleiha, situated on the ancient caravan route along the western edge of the Hajar mountains.

In 200 BC, the Persians, following an attack on the region, once more extended their influence right along the the western side of the Gulf, from Oman to Kuwait.

Major population migrations into the territory of the lower Gulf continued to establish settlement patterns for hundreds of years to come. In the 2nd century AD the Azdites, a tribal group of Qahtani extraction, moved north-eastwards from their homes in Yemen, dominating the south-western and western slopes of the Hajar mountain range by the 6th century, and leaving the eastern slopes of the Jebel al Akhdar and the Batinah to Sassanid (Persian) interests. From then on the predominant population flow into south-east Arabia was from the north, some of these migrants shared the Azdite (Qahtani) ancestry, others sprang from the Adnanian half of Arab genealogy. Although these major migrant groups dispersed in smaller units throughout the region, connections persisted between related family groups.

Persian influence continued in one form or another until 600 AD when the Prophet Muhammed despatched couriers to local tribes, seeking their support for his pan-Arab mission. The conversion of the local sun and fire-worshipping population to Islam was rapid and constituted the most profound and enduring spiritual and social revolution ever to have affected this area. From now on, Arab historians began to record more of the events occurring in southern Arabia. In the region of the UAE two major cities from this period, Dibba, facing the Gulf of Oman and Julfar, near Ras Al Khaimah were to flourish until well into the 17th century. Following the Prophet Muhammed's death, a revolt at Dibba led to a major confrontation (in 11 AH or 632 AD) between local tribes and the Muslim army during which thousands were killed: wave upon wave of simple stone monuments still mark the graves of the fallen in an extensive cemetery on the plain behind the town. This battle was a tremendous

Typical 2nd millennium BC beaker from Shimal is displayed at Ras Al Khaimah Museum. (Kay)

The triangular mountain at Shimal, with ancient settlement and necropolis at its foot. (Kay)

victory for the Mecca based army, from then on, the lower Gulf was firmly part of the Muslim World.

Throughout the major immigration movements and the radiation of the tribes across the entire region, the fundamental issue was, as it always has been, could the meagre economic resources of the area support the increasing population? Each individual tribal group was faced with the task of effective and efficient utilisation of its particular share of very limited resources. Even if climatic conditions were more favourable than today, one can safely assume that the indigenous people were required to develop a high level of versatility in order to exploit all the economic resources available, and that this factor did not change significantly over the centuries. The way in which these limited economic opportunities were utilised seems to have predetermined the intensely tribal structure of society, existing in its purest form right up until the discovery of oil. Camel-breeding, goat, sheep and cattle-rearing, cultivation on a small scale, fishing, pearling, trade by camel and ship, and crafts associated with these activities, were the major traditional means of earning a living in this difficult terrain. But economic circumstances changed continuously. In the last two millenia most tribes have at some stage experienced the bedouin existence and, at other times, sedentary life in villages and towns: bedouin tribes have taken possession of fertile areas and eventually come to work the soil themselves, on the other hand, settlers of drought-stricken areas have been driven into nomadism, eventually becoming desert Bedouin. But scarcity of resources in relation to population density also bred a highly characteristic adaptability of a more specific nature: the versatile tribesman. Frauke Heard-Bey succinctly described this pragmatic being as follows: "*He is to be found throughout the areas and throughout the ages. He spends the winter with his livestock in the desert and comes to the coast to fish in the summer in order to supplement his own and his animals' diet. He plants or harvests his dates and takes part in pearling or he sows and harvests his millet high up in the mountains and spends the hot months of the summer fishing at the coast, or he leads a caravan or steers a ship and then returns to engage in some quite different activity. In short, there have been at all times in this area not a few tribesmen, every one of whom knew all there was to know about camel-breeding, pearling, farming, fishing or sailmaking.*"

Iron Age village abandoned about 2,500 years ago at Hili, near Al Ain showing mud-brick walls which have remained intact, preserved by burial in sand. (Kay)

The tribal basis of society, remained indispensable in these difficult conditions until changed economic circumstances made it possible for an ever-increasing number of families to find a livelihood entirely from one economic activity. This was the situation even in the shaikdoms, such as Ras Al Khaimah and Sharjah, which were strongly orientated towards maritime trade.

Europe made its impact too on the lives of the indigenous population. Lorimer spoke of the lucrative trade in oriental luxuries to the West in the 15th century: "*It was evident that the discovery of some untrammelled line of access to India would confer great wealth and prestige on a nation able to profit by it*; *and the country which most earnestly devoted itself to the quest of a new way thither was Portugal.*" Vasco da Gama, aided by a famous Arab navigator Ibn Majid, reached India via Cape Horn, in August 1498. His achievement was to revolutionize trade between East and West. We know from Portuguese records that Alfonso de Albuquerque visited Dibba and Muscat in 1507, massacring local inhabitants, in a series of bloodthirsty attacks destined to seal the fate of any possible rapprochement between the Arabs and the Portuguese. Establishing forts at Dibba, Khor Fakkan, Muscat, Hormuz and Bahrain, the Portuguese maintained a repressive presence in the region until 1653. Duarte Barbarosa, writing in 1517, described Julfar (north of Ras Al Khaimah) as having '*persons of worth, great navigators and wholesale dealers. Here is a very great fishery as well, of seed pearls as of large pearls*; *and the Moors of Hormuz come hither to buy them and carry them to India and many other lands. The trade of this place brings in a great revenue to the King of Hormuz.*' But there was some cultural in-

2nd millennium B.C. long grave at Shimal, Ras Al Khaimah. (Kay)

The vast cemetery on the plain behind Dibba, presumed to be the remains of a decisive battle fought in A.H. 11 which established Islam in the Oman peninsula. (Kay)

terchange between these cruel interlopers and the local population, despite their abhorrent method of waging war on men, women and children—a practice at variance with Muslim tradition. Portuguese exploration of the Indian Ocean was made possible through the study of Arab navigational methods whilst the Arabs, in their turn, adapted the shape of local wooden dhows influenced by the square-sterned Portuguese Galleons.

British interest in the region grew steadily as internecine rivalry weakened the power of the tribal leaders. In contrast to Abu Dhabi, where the ruling family's position evolved within the cohesive and numerically superior confederation of the Bani Yas, the Qawasim, with power bases in a number of areas, including Ras Al Khaimah and Sharjah, were a clan which had succeeded in establishing its authority over a large number of different tribes. This highly distinctive and independent section of the Huwalah had, in the 18th century, earned a reputation as a strong naval power controlling the passage of vessels throughout the Straits of Hormuz enroute between Iraq and Oman and on to India, in spite of the opposition of the rulers of the the Persian coast and those of Oman. The Qawasim have been cast as the villanous pirates of the Gulf, a theme copper-fastened by Lorimer, official chronicler of the region at the turn of the century on behalf of the British presence in India, and propagated time and time again by historians quoting Lorimer as a basic source. Dr. Sultan al Qasimi, using the Bombay Archives opened in 1954, as his major fount for research material has thrown new light on the situation in his book, 'The Myth of Arab Piracy in the Gulf.'

"*Advocates of British imperialism have managed to propagate the notion that, towards the end of the eighteenth century and during the first two decades of the nineteenth century, Gulf Arabs were involved in a great scheme of piracy against international trade, not only in the Gulf, but also in the Red Sea, the Arabian Sea and the Indian Ocean. They argued that this sudden change on the part of the Gulf Arabs came about because these 'pirates' were encouraged and supported by the rising power of the Saudis whose creed the Gulf Arabs, particularly the Qawasim, had accepted with fervour. Supporters of this argument want us to believe that the Arabs of the Gulf were saved from this nefarious occupation by the benevolent efforts of the British East India Company, whose intervention in the Gulf was for the sole purpose of preserving law and order. The resulting British domination of the Gulf for almost two centuries was a responsibility thrust upon the British almost against their will. In my view, however, the East India Company was determined to increase its share of the trade of the Gulf by all possible means....The Company's Government of Bombay realised that any real opposition to their plans in the Gulf would come from the Qawasim.... In order to achieve this goal the decision-making bodies of the governments of Bombay and of India and indeed of the Empire itself, needed to be mobilised against the enemy. Accordingly, a concerted campaign was mounted by Company officials to present, or rather misrepresent, the Qawasim as pirates whose depredations posed a serious threat to all maritime activities in the Indian Ocean and adjacent waters. Any misfortune that happened to any*

Chinese porcelain dish of the 16th century AD from Julfar is displayed at Ras Al Khaimah Museum. (Kay)

ship in the area was capriciously attributed to the 'Joasmee pirates'.... The fight against 'piracy' became the Company's battle cry. If accidents did not occur, incidents were invented and attributed to these imaginary 'pirates'...."

In any event, a British naval expedition was despatched in 1819 from Bombay amongst a certain amount of controversy as to its military and political objectives. Commanded by Sir William Grant Keir, it did not stop at straightforward retribution and punishment of those who had attacked British shipping but set the scene for the retention of British influence in the area. The expedition culminated in an attack led on Ras Al Khaimah itself, during which the invading force set fire to many of the local dhows which they regarded as "pirate boats." A treaty was subsequently signed in January 1820 between the British and nine shaikhly rulers.

The present Rulers of the Emirates trace their ancestry back to the tribal leaders commanding the allegiance of their people in or around this tumultuous period. Abu Dhabi itself was founded in about 1761 following the chance discovery of a fresh-water source on the island by members of the Al Bu Falah sub-group of the Bani Yas during a hunting expedition from their home base in the oasis settlement of Liwa. In the late eighteenth century, the burgeoning island settlement, thriving on pearling and fishing, was selected as the tribal capital for the al Nahyan ruler, traditionally the leaders of the Bani Yas, who began construction of a fort around the water source. This impressive building, renovated to its former glory, still forms a focal point for the gleaming modern city of Abu Dhabi.

A small mosque at Bidiya on the east coast, said to be the oldest in the country. (Kay)

Even after the British established their political influence, the region's boundaries differed from those of today. It wasn't until the 19th century that Abu Dhabi extended its authority over the largest part of the Buraimi/Al Ain oasis. Gradually, by a process of lengthy diplomacy and a considerable amount of heated discussion, each emirate defined its borders. Ajman's and Umm Al-Quwain's were set in 1804. At that time Dubai and Abu Dhabi were linked as one. In 1833, following the accession of Shaikh Khalifa, great-grandfather of the present Ruler, Shaikh Zayed, to the leadership of the shaikdom of Abu Dhabi, Maktoum, an adviser to Shaikh Khalifa, moved to Dubai, occupied its fort, and, with the initial support of Sharjah, took control declaring a separate emirate of Dubai, which continued under the control of the Al Bu Falash section of the Bani Yas. The emirate of Fujairah was established in 1904, following a battle with the Ruler of Ras Al Khaimah. Next Sharjah and Ras Al Khaimah split into separate emirates, each led by a Qasimi ruler. Fujairah became an independent emirate in 1904, following a struggle with Ras Al Khaimah. There have been subsequent negotiations between various emirates, but this general picture has basically held firm.

The 19th century was a period of prosperity for some as the market for pearls expanded dramatically, leading to a marked increase in the settled population. But this relative flow of wealth was to dry up as the artificially cultured pearl gradually consumed an ever-diminishing market. By the 1950's population estimates in the Trucial States show a decrease in numbers of almost every tribe and coastal settlement as compared to the figures recorded by Lorimer. Emigration to find work in the oil industries of neighbouring countries played a major role in this pattern. However The UAE itself was shortly to benefit from the discovery and development of its own major petroleum resources — a factor which was to have a major impact on population densities in the region, as well as the structure and quality of the lives of the inhabitants. A substantial influx of immigrants has contributed enormously to the rise in numbers, but the country's indigenous population has also increased dramatically.

Intense negotiations between Bahrain, Qatar, and the present seven members of the UAE followed the British announcement in 1968 of its plans for a rapid withdrawal from the Gulf states for internal political reasons. Despite some initial hiccups in the arrangements, in December 1971, six emirates, Abu Dhabi, Dubai, Sharjah, Umm Al Quwain, Ajman and Fujairah were united by a provisional federal constitution into an internationally recognised political entity under the presidency of His Highness, Sheikh Zayed bin Sultan al Nahyan, Ruler of Abu Dhabi. The six were subsequently joined, early in 1972, by Ras Al Khaimah. The Rulers of all seven emirates form the Supreme Council, the foremost decision-making body of the federation. Whilst the individual emirates re-

Ruins of Falaya fort, Ras Al Khaimah, where the treaty with the British was signed in 1820. (Kay)

Stone weights such as these were used for weighing pearls. (Kay)

tain full sovereignty over their national resources, the central government has exclusive legislative and executive powers, not only in key areas such as foreign affairs and defence but also education and electricity, which in some other federations are under the regional authorities. Like all new states, the UAE has had its teething problems, but the stability and permanence of the federal structure has been reinforced by relative financial security and a gradual change of emphasis from regional to central administration. The UAE's very successful foreign policy, spearheading its high profile abroad, has also lent it considerable credibility at home, leading to the more rapid evolution of a national identity involving the transfer of tribal allegiance from local rulers to the UAE Government and its President.

The UAE has, in the past twenty years, accomplished an astounding metamorphosis from disparate desert enclaves to thriving modern state but, along the way, shepherded and shaped by Islam, it has not abandoned the traditions that have forged its strength and purpose.

THE PAST*

It is very early in the morning, let us say, fifty years ago. The little wooden **sambuk** lies at anchor alongside a pearl bank, some twenty miles offshore. There is not a ripple of wind. The sky is gently turning from black to dark blue. On the raised poop deck the **mutawwa** shakes himself free of the pile of old rags on which he has been sleeping, stands upright as still as the water for a moment, then turns his back on the lightening sky, 'Allahu Akbar!' his reedy voice echoes over the water. 'God is great. There is no god but Allah! And Muhammad is the messenger of Allah!' he calls to the fading stars. Below him on the deck bodies frowsty with sleep and salt stir into life. 'Come to prayer. Prayer is worthier than sleep!' Other voices raised in prayer can be heard through the darkness as the pearl divers rise to face another day among the oyster beds. The same scene could have occurred at almost any time before the advent of oil—fifty years, five hundred years, even (without the Muslim call to prayer) five thousand years ago.

The shaikhdoms of the United Arab Emirates cluster along the south-east shore of the Arabian Gulf. There are seven of them—Abu Dhabi, Dubai, Sharjah, Ras Al Khaimah, Fujairah, Ajman, Umm Al-Quwain, in order of size. Although there are distinctive, mainly tribal, differences between them, they are all conditioned by a harsh geographical combination of mountain, desert and sea. The mountains are the Hajar mountains, the backbone of Trucial Oman, created in a massive upheaval of continental plates that has left brown jagged folds and fissures of limestone and igneous rock, in certain places rich in fossils that reveal an earlier submarine existence. The sea is the Gulf, now torn by outsiders' quarrels. And the desert is the fringe of the Rub al-Khali, the great Empty Quarter of Arabia.

The mountains catch the rain off the Indian Ocean, very little of which falls on the land to the west of the mountains where the intermittent rainfall averages 136 mm a year. An average like that obscures the fact that some years there is none at all. Rain falling on the mountains, however, filters through to aquifers underlying the great gravel plain at the western foot of the mountains. Here some of the earliest signs of Man's existence in the region have been found in the flakes of flint found on outlying ridges of the mountains. As he learned to domesticate animals and grow crops, probably around the 4th to 3rd millennium BC (about 5,000 years ago), Man moved down on to the plain dependent on a temperamental run-off from the mountains after a rainstorm. Graves of the 3rd millenium BC found in these areas reveal in their contents a remarkably advanced way of life. Later, perhaps about 1000 BC, he began building **aflaj** (sing, **falaj**), the irrigation channels found all over this part of the world that run often for many miles below and then above ground eventually to water areas with reasonable topsoil to produce date palms, limes, fodder crops and perhaps a few vegetables. Such **aflaj** still run with water through the oases of Dhaid and Al Ain where remains of substantial settlements have been found.

Part of the coastline of the modern UAE falls east of the mountains along the Gulf of Oman. Here there is a narrow coastal plain, part of it belonging to the emirate of Fujairah, part belonging to Sharjah, filled with grey-green date palms until in the north, the mountains tumble straight into the sea at the Musandam peninsula which belongs to Oman. Most of the UAE is on the other, Gulf side of the mountains, south and west of the Musandam peninsula and the Hajar mountains with Ras Al Khaimah still with a moderate

Opposite

Mixing straw and mud to renovate Jahill fort, Al Ain. The fort was built in 1898 and is the birthplace of H.H. Sheikh Zayed, President of the UAE. (Kay)

**This chapter has been written by Sarah Searight*

Falaj irrigation channels distribute water through a palm grove at Hili, Al Ain. (Vine)

rainfall and enough surface runoff from the mountains to sustain agriculture, but with an ever more arid coast as one moves westwards. Along the way there are occasionally sheltered lagoons, as at Umm Al Quwain and Ajman, towns built on spits of sand the seaward side of lagoons where the fishing fleets could shelter from storms and raids; and creeks as at Ras Al Khaimah town, Sharjah and Dubai which gave even better shelter for larger vessels and, over the last hundred years, revived those trading contacts with the Indian subcontinent which were already flourishing five thousand years ago.

By the time Abu Dhabi is reached the coast has become a bleak expanse of salt flats (**sabkha**) and shallow inshore waters, dotted with sand banks and islands that barely rise above the blue saline waters of the Gulf. One of these islands contains Abu Dhabi town, now the capital of the federation; fifty years ago it used to muster one of the largest pearling fleets in the Gulf and some four hundred boats used to assemble every June in the lee of the island, near the present Al Maqta Bridge, before setting out for the pearling banks some ten to twenty miles out to sea to collect the precious oysters. But in these still shallow waters a far greater wealth had accumulated as tiny marine creatures and plants sank layer on layer, gradually transformed over millions of years from a sediment into the oil which has given rise in the last twenty years, to the startling sky line of Abu Dhabi town, rising now like a mirage from the summer haze.

The earliest signs of settled man in the Emirates come as something of a shock. He emerges from the darkness with such a flourish, mainly through tombs and their contents. The fineness of the construction and of some of the artefacts in several series of impressive tombs near the mountains have led archaeologists to wonder whether they might not be vestiges of the ancient civilisation of Magan mentioned in Sumerian documents as a source of copper, diorite, chlorite and other useful stones.

The oldest so far excavated are at Jebel Hafit

Dr Walid Yasin of Al Ain Department of Antiquities in the Iron Age Village of Hili. (Kay)

near Al-Ain, dating back to the 4th millennium, prior to 3000 BC. Others are at Qurn Bint Saud, a stark isolated mountain with a magnificent view over the stony plain a few miles east of Al Ain. Links with the outside world were first suspected at Umm an Nar, a site on the mainland shore by Abu Dhabi island where excellently constructed graves were found to contain fine pottery, beads, copper daggers and a pot with a hump-backed bull painted on it indicating possible links with the Indus valley or Baluchistan. A potsherd found later had the mark of a Mesopotamian seal on it. Presumably the artefacts were exchanged for pearls; the Sumerian story of Gilgamesh talks of the Flower of Immortality that grows on the seabed of the Gulf. Pearling was likely to have been as seasonal in the 3rd millennium BC as in the 20th century AD. Those who took part would have come down to the coast perhaps with their families and animals, with charcoal and firewood and dates, grown in the gardens of what are now Al Ain and Buraimi to add to the trade.

The Al Ain area is about two hundred kilometres inland from Abu Dhabi—three or four days' trek if one was bringing the family, according to elderly Abu Dhabians but possible in twenty-four hours if there was a raid (**ghazu**) in the offing. The track, now a six-lane highway, winds over the **sabkha** gradually rising into the sands until, between tall orange dunes, the great bulk of Jebel Hafit appears out of the haze and at its feet, spreading as far as the eye can see, the date gardens of Al Ain. These are watered by rainwater run-off from the Hajar mountains. Tombs and settlements excavated here, in particular around the gardens of Hili which contain some magnificient tombs again dating back to the 3rd millennium BC, indicate a remarkably well organised society, that could arrange the transport of building materials, construct such elegant structures and feed itself—judging by the contents of a refuse pit—with a diet rather more varied than their descendants of the early 20th century AD. This decline in the quality of diet may well have been because a once ample water table dropped, reducing agriculture to the subsistence level which preceded the discovery of oil. Part of that earlier prosperity may have been generated by the copper trade as extensive workings have been discovered in mines throughout the Hajar mountains, particularly in Wadi Jizzi.

Meanwhile evidence of continuous settlement since early prehistoric times, unique along the eastern littoral of the Arabian peninsula, is being

A Chlorite jar found in an excavated tomb at Wadi Qawr dates to the Iron Age, some time between 1100 and 500 BC (Kay)

accumulated by German archaeologists in Ras al-Khaimah. The settlement, generally thought to date from the 2nd millennium BC, is at Shimal, the name of the modern village which lies, with its date gardens, at the foot of the Hajar Mountains a few kilometres north of the town of Ras Al Khaimah. Rainfall in the mountains, heavier there than in any other part of the UAE, accounts for Shimal's modern date gardens. It also explains why vestiges of continuous settlement are now coming to light, mostly as graves resembling others previously excavated in the area, in particular their use for collective burials, but also including a settlement for perhaps as many as 6,000 inhabitants which, with their burial grounds, is thought to stretch some three kilometres along the base of the mountains. Low ribs of the mountains jut on to the plain protecting the inhabitants from attack by sea. The sea has since receded three or four kilometres, but shell beads and necklaces and numerous piles of discarded shells are evidence of the inhabitants' dependence on the sea for food and possibly livelihood. Some of the shell types are no longer found on local beaches today, only rarely among the few remaining mangroves.

Findings in the graves have included fine pottery, bones and arrowheads pointing to the middle of the 2nd millennium BC as a likely date for the settlement — 1600-1700 BC — but one grave was discovered to have two layers; here the 2nd millennium burial was overlaid by an Iron Age tomb which could have been built a thousand years later.

The livelihood can still only vaguely be delineated. Probably it was not so very different from life in Ras Al Khaimah in the pre-oil era. Houses seem to have had stone foundations, topped by palm frond, or **barasti**, walls and roofs. Date stones have been found, testifying to palm cultivation (the palm was cultivated from about the 4th millennium onwards) and bone finds indicate that the inhabitants probably kept goats, camels and perhaps even the humped zebu cattle, still seen wandering round the streets of Ras Al Khaimah city. Camels were domesticated in the 3rd millennium BC and it is conceivable that the people of Shimal were semi-nomadic, able to change grazing territory from time to time, much as the local people did until recently, able also to hunt the abundant wildlife, several species of which have since become nearly extinct.

Grave contents throw some light on possible contacts with the outside world, though in most cases robbers have been in before archaeologists and removed anything of value. Copper objects such as arrowheads and spearheads (two of these were found stuck in the ground outside one tomb, probably part of some burial ritual) could have come from a number of places in the Oman peninsula within a few days' camel ride from Shimal. Archaeologists have also been looking for a source of the soft grey stone, steatite, after finding quantities of finely turned and decorated steatite vessels in the graves.

Earlier excavations in one corner of Shimal turned up a small stone cube identified as a weight from Harappa in the Indus valley. Trade up and down the Gulf—from Mesopotamia, from the Indus valley, from places in between—was well established by the 2nd millennium BC and the archaeologists hope to find evidence of Shimal's involvement, possibly as an outlet for the raw materials of Magan—copper, various stones and charcoal. And clearly the inhabitants had water—probably run-off from the mountains—always a precious and attractive commodity for voyagers up and down the Gulf.

It is unlikely that life was ever easy in ancient Ras Al Khaimah. It seems, however, to have been better four thousands years ago than it was three thousand years ago. Pottery sherds of the second millenium show evidence of pots having been made on the wheel; those of the subsequent Iron Age are usually hand made. They also lack signs of having been cut from the clay by string, a neat and skilful way of removing the finished pot from the wheel still used by potters today. Was this a

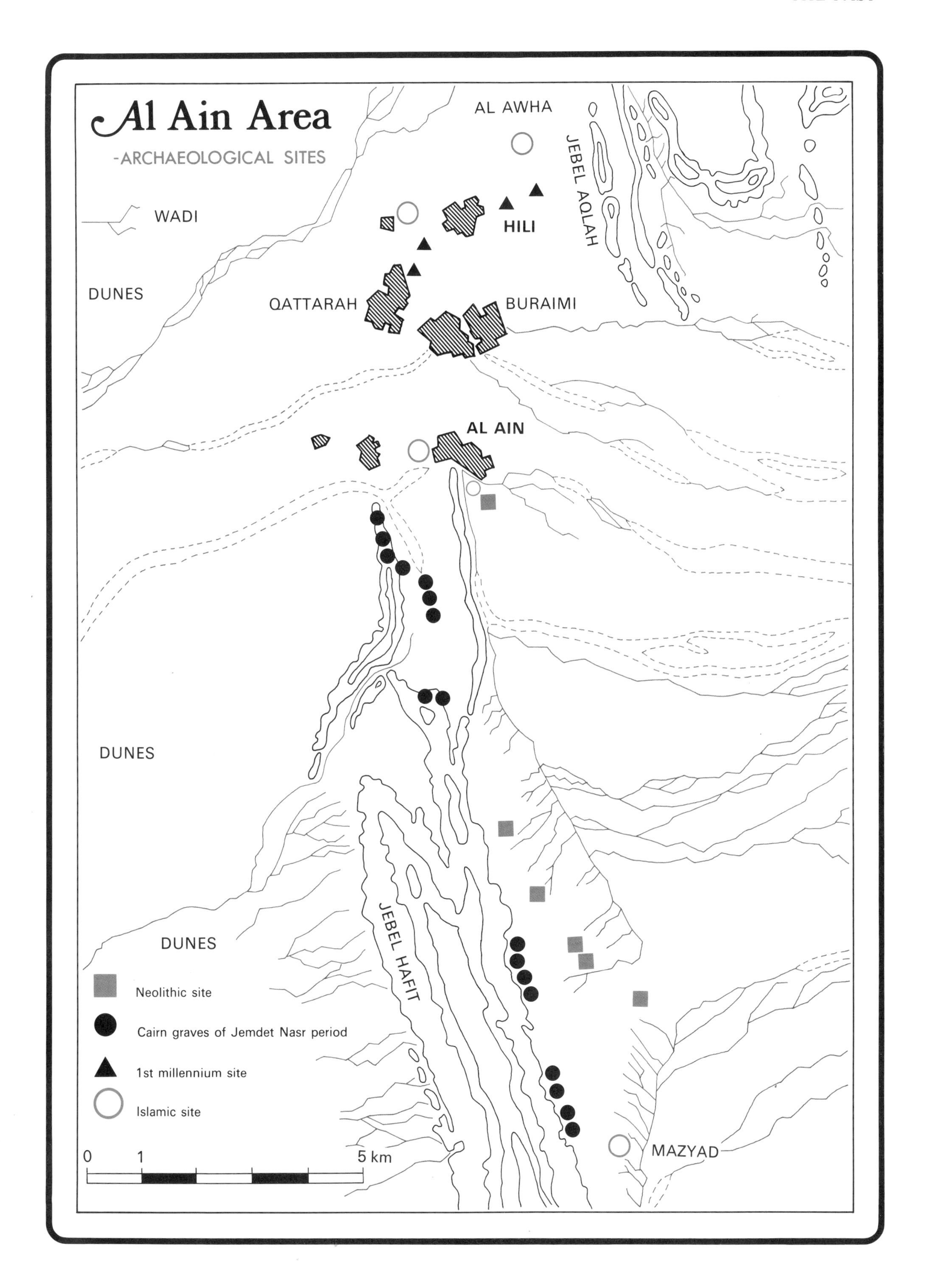
Al Ain Area
-ARCHAEOLOGICAL SITES
WADI
DUNES
AL AWHA
JEBEL AQLAH
HILI
QATTARAH
BURAIMI
AL AIN
DUNES
DUNES
JEBEL HAFIT
MAZYAD
Neolithic site
Cairn graves of Jemdet Nasr period
1st millennium site
Islamic site
0
1
5 km

sign of regression archaeologists are asking themselves. And if so, why? With scant evidence available archaeologists have a habit of posing more questions than they answer. But there are years of excavations ahead at so extensive a settlement as Shimal in which to fill in at least some of the blanks.

At all times water and its management were at the heart of survival in the region. The concept of the **falaj** is found in many parts of southern Arabia, Iran and Baluchistan—the engineering feat of bringing water over considerable distances with as little evaporation as possible. The longest **falaj** in the Al Ain area runs for over nine kilometres with a flow sufficient to irrigate many square miles of gardens. The organisation of its distribution was a political art so highly esteemed that the **falaj** warden was called the '**arif**', 'the knowing one'. Some **aflaj** in the emirates date from the Iron Age in the first millenium BC, watering villages whose numbers inland and along the coast indicate a surprisingly large population. Again the remains, mainly to do with burial, are the only enduring structures. People usually lived in houses made of **barasti**, only occasionally raising them on a rough stone base. Sadly for the modern archaeologist **barasti** has no staying power; though they were the principal type of habitation until the advent of oil wealth, only a few, scattered along the east coast, give an idea of what local people lived in for thousands of years. The graves sometimes compensate the excavator, in particular a 1st millennium BC burial site discovered two years ago [1986] at Qidfah in Fujairah on the east coast — 'a supermarket among graves!' exclaimed one archaeologist on seeing the contents. There were quantities of bronze bowls, arrowheads, bracelets, daggers, chlorite boxes and bowls and pottery, once again indicating an unsuspected affluence and contact with the outside world.

It is easy with hindsight, and given the present cosmopolitan population of the Emirates, to take for granted contacts with other civilisations in the region. It was much more astonishing when archaeologists first began excavating in the area, before the discovery of oil brought the Emirates to the international stage. It is also important to remember, when reading about the outside links, that the links with Arabia are far more real to the present population, reinforced by tribalism, Islam, and embodied seven years ago [1981] in the Gulf Cooperation Council.

Nowhere else in the Gulf is the tribal structure so important for an understanding of the UAE today; only through their tribal antecedents can one explain the present-day role of the federation's rulers and leading citizens. Tribes divide into sub-tribes, those divide into clans, those into families, the whole woven together into a remarkable tapestry of relationships tended by a consciousness of and love for genealogy. The territory over which a tribe moves is known as its **dirah** or **dar**, its rights to that territory are recognised by all and no other tribe may venture there without risking attack.

The tribal pattern of the UAE was probably established in the 2nd century AD. Traditional descriptions of migrations show that the great wastes of the Rub al-Khali were a less forbidding barrier to people accustomed to such conditions than they seem in a modern setting of international boundaries. Two major migrations into the area seem to have originated in South Arabia, probably Yemen. The first came via the Oman coast and through the Hajar mountains, reaching the Al Ain area around the second century AD;

This stone house with palm thatched roof was still in use as a temporary dwelling and farm building in 1988. Such classic examples of early artisinal architecture are fast disappearing in the UAE. Sha'am, Ras Al Khaimah. (Vine)

Remains of stone-built houses cloak the mountainside overlooking the village of Sha'am with its verdant palm groves along the north coast of Ras Al Khaimah. (Vine)

the other seems to have come via the Nejd and eastern Saudi Arabia, attracted also to the well watered and strategic oases of Al-Ain which controlled the passes to and from the coast. Later most of the population of the emirates became settled; true nomads have seldom numbered more than about ten per cent of the total population. The tribal structure, knit by tight kinship ties of marriage that kept usually substantial bridal dowries within the family, was well suited to the limited exploitation of scarce resources.

There are four main tribal groups in the emirate of Abu Dhabi. By far the most significant and most numerous are the Bani Yas, a loose federation of some fifteen tribes which dominates Abu Dhabi town, the string of scanty date gardens that make up the Liwa on the edge of the Rub al-Khali, and some of the Al Ain villages. Within this grouping of the Bani Yas there are several main tribes, each to some extent specialising in one aspect of the economy as well as predominating in one region. The Al Bu Falah traditionally provided the rulers of Abu Dhabi (now known as Al Nahyan), the first of the Bani Yas to acquire property in the Al Ain area. The Rumaithat (sing. al-Rumaithi) depended mostly on pearling and fishing. The Qubaisat (sing. al-Qubaisi) were prominent in the pearling fleets and also in the Liwa. Others are the Mazari (sing. al-Mazrui), the Sudan (sing. al-Suwaidi) and the Hawamil (sing. al-Hamali). There are also three other main tribes outside the Bani Yas. The Manasir (sing. al-Mansuri) are mainly in the al-Bhafra, the vast area controlling the territory bordering on Saudi Arabia. The Dhawahir (sing. al-Dhahiri) are mainly in the eastern part of the emirate. The Awamir (sing. al-Amiri) are mainly west of Buraimi, south of al-Dhafra.

Over several generations the Bani Yas extended its territory into the interior and particularly over the valuable date gardens of Al Ain. There are about a dozen villages in the Buraimi/Al Ain area of which Al Ain itself, Jimi, Hili, al-Qattarah, Mu'tirid, al-Muwaiji traditionally belonged to the Dhawahir and gave their allegiance to Abu Dhabi; the rest, inhabited by the Na'im, looked to Oman. In Al Ain the Bani Yas were able to exploit traditional disputes between the Na'im and the Dhawahir, the two principal tribes of the oases, coming to the rescue of the latter especially in fighting off several Wahhabi incursions in the first half of the 19th century and in return gradually acquiring date gardens to bolster their control. This was consolidated during the remarkably long rule of Shaikh Zayed bin Khalifah Al Bu Falah between 1855 and 1909. There was increasing coming and going between Abu Dhabi town on the coast and Buraimi, especially during the summer—whole families coming down to the coast in May for the pearling season and returning to Al-Ain in time for the date harvest. Abu Dhabi island has been the headquarters of Abu Dhabi's rulers although important members of the family have traditionally been despatched to maintain its control of other areas.

This domination of Al Ain by the Bani Yas, coinciding with their growing prosperity from pearling, meant they had less time for tending their much poorer palms in the Liwa. There were estimated to be forty-two little settlements in the Liwa in the early 1950s, most of them only occupied for the date harvest in the mid-summer when up to three thousand people might be camped around the palms. In recent years, however, the proximity of the Liwa to Saudi Arabia and the importance of maintaining international borders because of oil production has led to considerable sums of development money being spent in the western area. The present ruler Shaikh Zayed bin Sultan al Nahyan is surrounded in Abu Dhabi town, now the capital of the federation, by the formalised hierarchy of a semi-modern administration, much of it made up of foreigners. But the maintenance of that web of tribal relationships is as important as ever and for long spells, often in the summer, he goes off to the western region to spend time with the local tribes, leaving generous donations for wells, pumps, pick-up trucks and even a falcon or two when he goes. Vast areas of the western region have now been planted with trees.

Large glazed jar of about 2nd century BC from Mleiha (Al Ain Museum). (Kay)

Dubai presents a very different picture, tribally more homogeneous with a large foreign element in its population. It was established by a breakaway branch of the Bani Yas, the Al Bu Falasah, in 1833. Relations with Abu Dhabi's Al Bu Falah have not always been easy and the two tribes were intermittently at war from 1945-48, in the lifetime of the two present rulers. Against such a background the staying power of the federation often seems remarkable. Dubai's location along one of the best harbours to be found on the littoral of the Arabian Gulf, the foresight of its al Maktoum rulers and a community of astute merchants, have all contributed to Dubai's economic success. Although dominated locally by the Al Bu Falasha, it has also accommodated a genuinely cosmopolitan population of Baluchis, Persians and Indians who have helped to foster an appreciation of Dubai's geographical location in the region and the importance of regional trading links, which have stood it in good stead for most of this century.

The country north of Dubai is dominated by the 'multi-tribal' Qasimi (plural Qawasim) empire. The Qawasim are a clan of the Huwalah tribe which in the eighteenth century occupied ports on both sides of the Gulf, with their main base on the well-defended creek of Ras Al Khaimah. Their interest lay in the sea and the trade that sailed

Fine glazed jar from Ad Dour, 1st century AD (Kay)

upon it. They regarded the waters of the lower Gulf as their territory in much the same way as other tribes dominated certain areas of the hinterland; those who intruded upon it were fair game for raids. The intruders came mostly from the Indian subcontinent, seen by the British as under their protection; moreover the British thought of the Gulf as one of the principal routes of communication between India and Britain and disliked any activity that might cause an interruption of the route. To the Qawasim the British and their allies were conspicuously foreign intruders in Muslim waters.

On several occasions the British raided and ultimately destroyed the fleets lying up the creek of Ras Al Khaimah and elsewhere on the coast. They were not concerned, however, with the Qasimi domination of the hinterland. Ever since an ex-ruler of Sharajh, Salim bin Sultan, installed himself as ruler of Ras Al Khaimah, in 1910, the Al Qasimi clan has been split into two branches—one continuing to rule Sharjah and the other ruling Ras Al Khaimah. Salim bin Sultan's grandson, Shaikh Saqr bin Muhammad al-Qasimi, has been ruler since 1948.

North of a line between Sharjah town on the Gulf coast and Khor Kalba on the east coast and south of the hostile Musandam peninsula, the Sharqiyin are by far the most numerous tribe, second in numbers in the UAE only to the Bani Yas. They are strongest to the east of the Hajar mountains, along the dramatically narrow and starkly beautiful coastal plain where they planted their prolific date gardens, with their main base at Fujairah. Although ruled as an independent shaikhdom since the middle of the nineteenth century, Fujairah was only recognised as such in 1952 when concessions were sought for oil exploration. It is the most remote of the emirates and also the least developed; the Sharqiyin have been more inclined to stay at home rather than migrate to the affluent oil developments elsewhere in the country. Recently it has tried, with moderate success, to exploit its position outside the tempestuous waters of the Gulf proper, establishing a port on the major shipping routes of the world, the safer side of the Straits of Hormuz.

On the Gulf side of the mountains two other shaikhdoms have maintained a quasi-independence of their Qasimi overlords. In Umm Al Quwain the Al Ali is the predominant tribe, based mainly in the town of Umm Al Quwain which sits on a spit of sand overlooking a lagoon where fishing boats and a few pearling boats used to bring in a small income for the ruling family of al-Mu'alla. Along the road towards Dubai, Ajman is ruled by a branch of the Na'im of Buraimi.

Life in the emirates in these tribal, pre-oil times was dependent on three elements. These were water, the camel and the date. Above all it was ordered and disciplined according to the tenets of Islam. Islam came to the region probably in the second half of the seventh century AD. It offered a sense of order, security and justice where these had not been easily found before and it became a unifying force, an 'indestructible lasting fabric' in a world where the harsh impermanence of life seemed all-pervading. Despite the changes of the last twenty years the people of the Emirates feel as deeply as ever a universal identification with the spirit of Islam, evoked without hypocrisy in greetings and farewells, conversation on the happenings of the world, commiserations and congratulations. Prayer times, called out from the many mosques that have been built with revenues from oil production, impose a rhythm on the day, Muslim holidays impose it on the year. Everyone aspires to perform the **haj**, the pilgrimage to Mecca, obligatory at least once in a lifetime and feasible in these days of improved communications. Alms giving, **zakat**, is re-enacted in the great generosity of wealthy oil producing countries such as the UAE to other less fortunate Muslim countries. Ramadhan, the Muslim period of fasting, is welcomed by people who see it as a respite from the abundance of modern life. Such a faith was well suited to people living at subsistence level, engendering a resignation to their meagre livelihood dependent on such relatively basic essentials as the camel and the date - and water, essential to the consumer as well as to his meagre food crops and his animals.

Date cultivation is the oldest form of agriculture in the area. Dates are best in Ras Al Khaimah, most prolific in Al Ain and Fujairah. They are eaten fresh or dried, kept for many months until the next harvest, and used to be taken out to sea on the pearling boats. They are also boiled down into a syrup into which one dips torn off strips of wafer-thin bread for breakfast. They are produced whenever a guest comes to call, a certain expertise called for in flipping the stone out before putting it in one's mouth. They can also be fed to animals; goats are particularly partial to them. The leaves of the date palm were woven into the walls of the **barasti** hut, the trunks supported the roofs of fortifications.

Young Sudanese camel herdsman practising some circus tricks. (Vine)

There is a 5,000-year old carving of that other mainstay of life, a camel, on a tomb at Umm al-Nar but this is likely to have been a wild camel; domestication probably occurred about four thousand years ago. The camel soon spread across Arabia and into Africa, Mesopotamia and India, often used to carry incense, salt or dates along the ancient trading routes that crisscrossed so much of the peninsula. The Quran speaks of it with great respect and camels carried its Arab missionaries into Africa, Syria, Mesopotamia and even Spain. In the old days the camel was valued first for its milk - together with dates a dietary staple and still popular today (it is full of Vitamin C) - then for its carrying ability and finally for its body. Camel's meat was and still is also highly valued and there is plenty of it these days. Other commercial bits of the beast were its hump - boiled down to extract the fat; its dung - dried and used for fuel; its wool - woven into rugs and harnesses.

The camel's quality, however, was often likely to be rated by its speed in the **ghazu** or raid. Life as we have seen was extremely harsh - older Abu Dhabians still recall the sheer hunger of their youth - and as the earlier description of tribal relationships demonstrates squabbles over fishing or pearling rights or, more often, over wells and date palms easily welled up into raids and bloodshed. The **ghazu** was part of life, some occasions more serious than others, not always involving great loss of life but contributing to a sense of insecurity already engendered by an existence on the fringe of subsistence. In the 19th century this insecurity was aggravated by a succession of Wahhabi incursions from central Arabia into the much envied date gardens of Al-Ain and Buraimi. Nowadays

Camel-talk preoccupies the owners. (Vine)

A look-out fort near Hatta. (Vine).

the forts are a picturesque reminder of that embattled past, their survival a tribute to their sturdy construction. Archaeologists have even unearthed defences at Rumailah in Al-Ain dating back to the first millenium BC. Several forts have been restored not only as reminders of a different past, but also as a repositories for other historical links.

Each of the emirates has a main town on the coast - Abu Dhabi and Dubai, Sharjah, Ajman, Umm Al Quwain, Ras Al Khaimah and round the corner on the shores of the Indian Ocean, Fujairah. Abu Dhabi town was built on an island, separated from the mainland by a creek that could be forded at low tide. The creek was defended by a small lookout tower, Al-Maqta, half way across, the island by a substantial fort. Dubai, Sharjah, Ajman, Umm Al Quwain and Ras Al Khaimah were all built along creeks offering sheltered harbours that needed to be protected. Fujairah's shore is more exposed and had even more need of protection; indeed it was one of the last emirates to have seen fighting, in 1972 over the ownership of an oasis which was disputed by Sharjah. Of these, only Sharjah's fort has virtually disappeared; the rest have all undergone, or are undergoing, some degree of restoration. Each was once the seat and administrative base of the ruler.

Wealth in the Trucial States before pearling and oil was based partly on date gardens, partly on flocks of animals, mainly goats and camels. Fortifications were built to protect these and the routes between them. They were also places where the people could come to the ruler with grievances or requests. And they were centres of local government. The most impressive of forts protecting date gardens are in the villages of the Al Ain and Buraimi oases that now lie in the UAE and Oman. There are generally reckoned to be nine such villages, six of them belonging to Abu Dhabi, three to Buraimi, as well as a number of less significant forts amongst the date gardens. Dhaid oasis in Sharjah contained a substantial fortress over its main **falaj** and others south of the town, now mostly disappeared. Mountain passes such as that between Dubai and the Indian Ocean coast at Fujairah also needed defences, one of the most picturesque in these more peaceful days being at Bithna, once on the main wadi track through the mountains, now just off the two-lane highway that has replaced it. Wells, now sometimes abandoned, were guarded by diminutive forts such as those in the Liwa and also in Ras Al Khaimah at Al-Khatt, a large oasis with substantial wells at the foot of the mountains. Most of those in the Liwa

Old Fahidi fort of Dubai which now houses the museum. (Kay)

are ruined almost to the point of having disappeared, several of them destroyed long ago in fighting between Abu Dhabi and Qatar in the 1880s.

The forts have a simple nobility in contrast with the elaborate modern structures which often overshadow them today. They reflect the influences that have passed over the Arabian peninsula through the generations - Central Arabian, Yemeni, Iranian, contacts with India and the Indian Ocean, finally the Portuguese; some architectural historians argue that European fortifications, including the Portuguese, were themselves influenced by Arab architecture as discovered during the Crusades. The Portuguese found forts at Ras al-Khaimah and Khor Fakkan when they arrived in the early sixteenth century.

The grandest of the UAE forts today is that of Abu Dhabi which has been well and lavishly restored. The Bani Yas are said first to have discovered water on Abu Dhabi island about 1761, thereafter making it their main seat. A modest fort which was first built at the end of the 18th century was extensively enlarged in the 1920s and 1930s during the years of pearling prosperity. It dominated the local seasonal community of pearl divers although its earlier importance has now been crowded out by the surrounding office and apartment blocks. Today the oldest part is the round tower near the western wall. A fussy screen wall now surrounds it but if you squeeze between curtain wall and inner wall you capture a sense of scale and coolness that must have been impressive attributes of the pre-boom fort. The fort is now being used to house the Centre for Documentation and Research, an archive of the federation's earlier history well suited to preservation in such a building.

Dubai's Fahidi Fort has seen many lives - residence, arsenal, jail and now museum, one of the best in the emirates. The town is mainly on the west side of the creek; Deira opposite is now linked by bridges and a tunnel. The fount of so much Gulf knowledge, J.G. Lorimer, writing at the beginning of this century, noted a local theory that Dubai fort was built on the remains of a Portuguese fort. The museum reflects the emirate's fortunes over the last hundred and fifty years - its pearling past, early photographs of the creek, the development of the modern entrepot. Further along the coast Ajman is just completing the restoration of its fort and Ras Al Khaimah has also just turned its main fort into a museum. Numerous look-out towers still guard the coast between Ras Al Khaimah and Umm Al Quwain, a reminder of a bellicose heritage.

The almost consistently bad relations between the Dhawahir and Na'im tribes in the past accounts for many of the fortifications still visible in Al Ain today. Others were built during the Wahhabi incursions that took place on a number of occasions between 1800 and 1869 when the Wahhabis finally withdrew. The Wahhabis take their name from Muhammad bin Abd al-Wahhb, a religious reformer who lived in central Arabia in the 18th century. He won support for his campaign for a return to a purer Islam from the Al Saud family in the Nejd and, in the early 19th century, his adherents began pouring out of central Arabia into surrounding regions including Al Ain's prosperous date plantations.

Today Al Ain is the cultural heart of the UAE. Not only does it contain the Emirates University but there are also many links with this very different past. Of these links the forts, glimpsed among the date gardens or out in the desert watching over approach roads, are the visible reminders of a more turbulent past. Several have been, or are being, restored by the Abu Dhabi Department of Antiquities. One fort, Qasr Sultan, is alongside the excellent little museum that houses archaeological and ethnological remains. Another particularly well restored fort is outside the oasis at Mazyad, beneath that strange impressive slab of mountain, Jebel Hafit. The wall of rock, the sands disappearing into the heat haze which usually totally obliterates the Hajar mountains, whence comes the vital water for the oasis, a gentle but abundant **falaj** flowing through the Mazyad experimental farm, is an extraordinarily 'Beau Geste' setting for this delightful fort. A substantial gateway leads through thick walls to the shady courtyard, rather more overgrown today than it probably was when it served as a pen for domestic animals. The courtyard is surrounded by rooms like a caravanserai; stairs lead up to their roofs and the corner towers.

One of these towers contains a well ventilated **majlis**, with a small window opening to catch the afternoon breeze. I have often thought, sitting at that window in the late afternoon in summer, how restorative it must have been when the pearl diving season ended and the boat crews came ashore, sorted out their gains and losses, collected up those families that had come to the coast for the season and headed inland, a hot dreary trudge but worth it to return to the shade of the palms, the

The renovated fort of Ras Al Khaimah now houses an attractive museum. The oldest tower of the fort is thought to have formed part of the town's defences. (Kay)

A coastal watch-tower stands on a slight rise above the main road, as one approaches Ras Al Khaimah from the south. Such watch-towers formed an essential element in local defences right up to the early part of this century. (Vine)

trickle of fresh water, the rhythmic beat of cicadas drumming through the evening prayer. The contrast between coast and interior is best appreciated in summer, even in these days of air-conditioning, when the humidity of the coast becomes almost unbearable.

In the early part of the 19th century the activities of the Qawasim in trying to establish control over the seas of the lower Gulf and harassing traders attracted the attention of the British. The British had been interested in the Gulf since the 17th century, when the East India Company realised that Persia might be a better market for English goods - mainly woollen fabrics - than India and gradually ousted the Portuguese from their earlier monopoly of Gulf trade. Anarchy in Persia throughout much of the 18th century reduced the trade to a trickle and the Company had cut down drastically on its factories on the Persian shore and at Basra. In 1798, however, Napoleon's invasion of Egypt, designed to cut British communications with India and even lead to a revival of French fortunes in India, exposed the vulnerability of British links with such valuable possessions. The Gulf now came to be seen as the most vital of those links and a few months after Napoleon's invasion the East India Company had concluded a treaty with the Sultan of Muscat, an important refuge and watering place in the Indian Ocean, in which he undertook not to aid the French.

By 1810 the French were no longer a menace in this part of the world but Indian as well as British shipping was facing a new problem - that of raids by Qawasim 'pirates'. The British despatched a small punitive expedition in 1809-10, storming and taking a fort on the coast of the Gulf of Oman. It had little effect on the raids, however, which grew even fiercer and led to a second expedition in 1819 against Ras Al Khaimah. This time the Qasimi fleets were destroyed and the Qawasim made to sign a treaty foreswearing piracy. The shaikhs of Abu Dhabi and Bahrain, not considered as pirates, nevertheless were signatories to the treaty, the enforcement of which became the responsibility of the British Political Resident in Bushire.

The British were mainly concerned to preserve a maritime peace and took little interest for many years in the interior. In the 1830s they became involved in a war between the Al Bu Falah and the Qawasim which led to pearl banks being abandoned, herds depleted, plantations destroyed. The war eventually moved out to sea, hence the British involvement. In 1835 the British Political Resident, Captain Samuel Hennell, recommended a truce on the pearl banks which was reviewed annually until 1843. Then it was signed for the next ten years and finally, in 1853, replaced by the Perpetual Treaty of Maritime Peace. Thus the area became known as the Trucial Coast.

Throughout the 19th century the British were chiefly concerned to maintain the freedom and safety of the Gulf water way for their vessels and those of Indian traders. As far as possible they excluded other European powers from developing political or economic links with the region but the affairs of the hinterland were not generally considered part of the Political Resident's responsibilities. From time to time the rivalries of the shaikhs impinged on the maritime peace and such activities as gun-running to the tribes of Baluchistan and Afghanistan led to stern rebukes from the Resident and raids on local shipping by British war vessels. It also suited the shaikhs sometimes to claim to be under British protection, especially when faced with the Wahhabi menace. Indian residents of Gulf towns sometimes came under at-

Solitary watch-tower in Wadi Helu is one of many such towers to be seen throughout the UAE where they were once used to guard villages and palm groves. (Kay)

tack, particularly during the final Wahhabi occupation of Buraimi between 1853 and 1869, again resulting in British threats to the raiders. But the threats seldom needed to amount to more serious action.

British agents in Bushire, Muscat and sometimes elsewhere travelled to the various coastal settlements and Buraimi, their reports to the government in India the best historical and virtually only written record of the period. Relative tranquillity was established in the interior during the long rule of Shaikh Zayed bin Khalifah in the latter part of the nineteenth century, his influence, according to Percy Cox (British Resident in Muscat at the time), was '*almost invariably exercised in the interests of general peace*'. He also established the military authority of the Al Bu Falah over the other shaikhdoms, maintained after his death by the powerful wealth of the pearling banks.

Peace had in this case coincided with fashion; the necks and ears of European and American ladies in the nineteenth and early twentieth centuries were becoming ever more heavily decorated with lustrous pearls and the Maritime Truce established a relative tranquillity within which trading could flourish. Pearl banks are all along the Arabian littoral, mainly a few miles offshore. But the best lie in the great bay of the Gulf between Qatar and the Musandam peninsula, eight to twelve fathoms deep. The banks were common property, although in the nineteenth century the British government of India decreed that the pearl fisheries were to be restricted to the inhabitants of the Gulf. The peak of the fisheries was reached in the years immediately before and after World War I. By 1920 Abu Dhabi had the largest pearling fleet in the lower Gulf - around four hundred boats. With the boom in the demand for pearls at the turn of the century some 22,000 of the Trucial Coast's population, 74,000 in the Gulf as a whole, depended on the seasonal haul for purchasing power. Local pearling merchants acquired considerable influence because of the relative affluence. Dubai came to replace Bahrain (and Lingeh on the Iranian coast) as the local pearl trading centre thus establishing itself on the road to prosperity.

The decline of the Gulf's pearl fisheries stemmed from the economic depression which hit Europe and the United States in the 1930s. No one could afford real pearls any more. About the same time the Japanese discovered how to make cultured pearls by introducing an artificial body into the mollusc. It was a fatal combination for the Gulf pearl and its fishermen. Today almost all pearls are cultured - 70 per cent of them from Japan. The last pearling fleets were finally disbanded soon after World War II although boats were still going out from the Emirates long after they had been beached elsewhere; pearling there remained the only means of livelihood where others more fortunate had found oil.

The UAE came late to the discovery and exploitation of oil. The first oil concession agreement was signed in Abu Dhabi fifty years ago, in 1939. It was another twenty-three years, however, before any revenue was earned from oil. Nowadays the existence of oil and the wealth it has brought to the country is taken for granted, as are all the amenities it has paid for. But in those early days its existence was far from assured and the amenities conspicuously absent. The population of the Emirates actually declined in the years immediately after the war as its inhabitants left to look for a living elsewhere.

Oil seepages in Iraq and Iran had been known for thousands of years and foreign companies had been exploiting them from the early years of the

Fort at Al Ain now houses the Al Ain Museum. (Vine)

twentieth century. Competition between companies and consuming countries soon entered the picture, particularly after World War I; the British Navy had converted to oil just before the war and they, like others, were looking for security of supplies.

Early in the 1930s the D'Arcy Exploration Company, the major shareholder in the Anglo-Persian Oil Company which had been exploiting oil reserves in southern Persia since the early 20th century, obtained options to explore for oil from most rulers of the Trucial Coast, Qatar and Oman. At the time the rulers were under British protection, under the terms of the Perpetual Maritime Truce. The options included no obligation to look for oil but prevented any other company from doing so. In 1935 the Iraq Petroleum Company, a consortium of British, American, French, Dutch and other interests, founded a subsidiary, Petroleum Concessions Ltd, with an office in Bahrain to handle all concessionary affairs in the Gulf. A year later Petroleum Concessions formed Petroleum Development (Trucial Coast) to take over the D'Arcy options. PD (TC) immediately began negotiating for concessions. Despite a certain reluctance to admit foreigners to the interior of the emirates, most rulers were all too conscious of the economic decline of their one source of income - pearls - and were looking for an alternative source.

World demand for oil at this point was not great. Increasing demand after World War II could easily be met by expanding development and production from existing fields. Moreover oil rigs were in short supply and foreign oil companies were reluctant to use available expertise and equipment on new ventures. Nevertheless, immediately after the war during the winter of 1946/7, geologists and geophysicists began surveying in many parts of Abu Dhabi, the most likely part of the Trucial Coast, for oil both on and offshore, because of its position on the Gulf geosyncline and its proximity to heavy oil-bearing structures elsewhere in Kuwait, Saudi Arabia, Bahrain and Qatar.

The coast between Abu Dhabi and Dubai is mostly low-lying salt flats and shallow inshore waters. An onshore location, Ras Sadr, was chosen near Abu Dhabi, one of the few places on the coast with water deep enough to land stores, equipment, materials and supplies from all directions. A consortium of British and French and later Japanese interests, combined in Abu Dhabi Marine Areas, began exploring offshore from the minute Das Island. Oil was struck in the middle of the desert at Bu Hasa in 1959 and exports began from Jebel Dhanna in the western region of Abu Dhabi emirate in 1963. Offshore oil was struck in commercial quantities in 1960 and exports began from Das Island in 1962. Oil was discovered offshore in Dubai in 1966 and exports started up in 1969; an onshore field was discovered at Margham in 1980. Sharjah found oil on Abu Musa island which it has to share with Iran, exporting from 1974, as well as an onshore field at Sajaa in 1980; and Ras Al Khaimah found a small offshore field in 1983.

The Emirates' oil and gas reserves are among the largest in the world. Proven oil reserves at the end of 1985 totalled a staggering 31 billion barrels. That is enough for the next eighty years at current rates of production. Proven natural gas reserves total nearly 35 trillion cubic feet. By far the largest portion of these reserves is in Abu Dhabi. There are three main onshore fields - Asab, Bu Hasa and Shah - and three main offshore fields - Umm Shaif, Lower Zakum and most recently Upper Zakum. There are also a number of smaller offshore fields. Dubai has oil in smaller quantities, both offshore and now also onshore; Sharjah is in much the same position although with yet smaller fields. The other emirates are still living on their hopes but have meanwhile benefited from the largesse stemming from the good fortune of Abu Dhabi. Production in 1987 was well over a million barrels a day, of which around 800,000 barrels were produced by Abu Dhabi.

When the oil first began to flow in the 1960s, the natural gas which came out of the ground in association with the oil was flared off at the wellhead. Flying down the Gulf was an extraordinary experience, lit by giant torch after giant torch. Today the only substantial flare left is at Sharjah's Sajaa field and that is diminishing, with the gas being extracted, piped to fractionation plants or liquid petroleum plants and used in an increasing variety of ways. Huge quantities of Abu Dhabi's offshore gas are exported from Das Island to Japan for Tokyo Electric. Onshore gas is used either for local power generation and desalination or piped to Abu Dhabi's industrial centre at Ruwais.

Abu Dhabi is the only Gulf oil producer not to have claimed 100 per cent ownership of its oil industry. A national oil Company, Abu Dhabi National Oil Company, was set up in November 1971, acquired stakes in offshore and onshore producing companies the following year, to a controlling share by 1973 of 60 per cent. The partners in the original concessions are still partners, though with much reduced shares.

The impact of oil wealth on local life has, of course, been revolutionary, with oil revenue rising to a peak of $18.5 billion in 1980, the population increasing nearly 100 per cent in the 1970s and another 50 per cent in the 1980s to 1.6 million.. Yet as with most revolutions there is a reassuring element of continuity. In twenty-five years the infrastructure and superstructure of 20th century life has been established. A teenager exclaimed at Abu Dhabi, 'Why, it's the same age as I am!' And of course the newness of the environment is its striking feature. Within this newness health, education, communications, water are the most conspicuous improvements, made possible not only by lavish injections of oil revenues but also by the armies of expatriates who now form some 80 per cent of the population. This has been the most worrisome aspect of modernisation for the local people who fear the undermining of their traditions, their religion, their raison d'etre by so many foreigners. Yet they have behaved with great generosity and tolerance to those visitors, many of whom have been able considerably to improve their own standard of living thanks to their employment in the Gulf. Attitudes are still conditioned by the same Muslim, tribal desert code as before.

As if coping with such sudden affluence were not enough in itself, the Emirates have also over the last fifteen years had to develop a political entity. Hard on the heels of the first influx of oil revenues came the British announcement in 1968 of their pending withdrawal from political and military commitments in the Gulf. The decision came as an unpleasant surprise to the Gulf shaikhdoms. The main inspiration for constructing a federation as an alternative to the British presence came from two neighbouring shaikhs, Shaikh Zayed bin Sultan al Nahyan of Abu Dhabi who had taken over from his older brother Shaikh Shakhbut bin Sultan in 1966, and Shaikh Rashid bin Said al Maktoum of Dubai. Negotiating to replace the British presence with federation was not easy and involved the burying of many hatchets. The discussions lasted three years, starting with a federal agreement between Abu Dhabi and Dubai, discussing but ultimately discarding the possibility of a nine member federation which would have included Qatar and Bahrain and finally declaring the establishment of a six-member federation in December 1971. Ras Al Khaimah, anxious that the smaller poorer emirates should be equal partners of the rich, eventually joined in February 1972.

The ties that bind the federation are necessarily loose. The federal government has little muscle as yet and individual rulers have often more authority in their emirates than federal ministers. Areas of sovereignty which were not assigned under the constitution to the UAE government have remained in the hands of individual emirates - most conspicuously in the areas of natural resources and defence - which still resist any infringement of their autonomy. UAE oil production for instance frequently exceeds its OPEC quota because Dubai regards its oil production as its own affair.

Abu Dhabi is the capital and seat of government but traditional methods of government are often preferred, as in a ruler's **majlis**. This is an informal gathering, based on the Arabic word for 'sitting', at which anyone may feel free to call on the ruler, express an opinion, make a complaint or a request and the ruler likewise make his feelings and policies known. Until he fell ill several years ago Shaikh Rashid, ruler of Dubai, went to his **majlis** early every morning to receive visitors. In the smaller Emirates - Ajman, Umm Al Quwain, Fujairah, Ras al-Khaimah for instance - locals feel quite at ease dropping in on their ruler and asking for his help, offering him their advice or just passing the time of day.

The president of the UAE and the moving force behind the federation is Shaikh Zayed bin Sultan al Nahyan. Both Shaikh Zayed and Shaikh Rashid, Vice President and Prime Minister, were reconfirmed in their positions in October 1986, a five-yearly event which also involves the renewal of the provisional federal constitution. The constitution is likely to remain provisional for the foreseeable future, allowing for flexibility in inter-emirate dealings but, in other respects, acknowledging the difficulty of melding into one, such disparate and often hostile units, Shaikh Rashid has been ill for several years now and the running of Dubai emirate is the responsibility of his three sons: Shaikh Maktoum who is also Crown Prince of Dubai, Shaikh Hamdan (federal minister of finance) and Shaikh Muhammad (federal minister of defence). Shaikh Zayed also prefers to leave much of the day-by-day running of Abu Dhabi's affairs to his eldest son Crown Prince Shaikh Khalifa who is also deputy commander-in-chief of the country's armed forces. The highest authority in the federation belongs to the Supreme Council, consisting of the seven rulers, which meets once or twice a year. There is also a federal National Council consisting of forty members nominated from the various emirates by the Rulers, mainly on a tribal or family basis.

The federation is matched in regional politics by the Gulf Cooperation Council (GCC), founded in 1981 to face the challenge of the Iran-Iraq war. Its members are the UAE, Saudi Arabia, Kuwait, Bahrain, Qatar and Oman. The GCC has enabled Gulf leaders and officials to get to know each other in all sorts of economic and cultural fields, a dramatic change from the hostility which often governed their relations in the past.

Acacias cling to sand-dunes at the base of sedimentary folds in the mountains behind Rams in northern Ras Al Khaimah. (Vine)

NATURAL HISTORY

To many people, the desert appears to be little more than a waterless waste-land where few species survive. Flying over the Arabian peninsula, gazing down from the air- conditioned comfort of a modern airliner, one is greeted by seemingly endless vistas of wilderness whose only identifiable features are deeply indented rugged valleys, stark hills and endless rolling dunes. At ground-level, however, a different story emerges for, contrary to popular belief, a diverse assemblage of plants and animals do live here, each adapted to overcome the stress exerted by extreme temperature ranges, and the scarcity of that essential life-giving element, water. Here, if one pauses long enough to look closely, one will discover plants capable of existing on the moisture of morning dew, and a whole host of insects, reptiles, birds and mammals for whom the deserts of southern Arabia are their chosen home.

The Arabs of course, have lived amongst this wildlife for hundreds of years and are adept at locating animals or utilising plants in the desert environment. The native ability to track animals is quite uncanny, as contributor Linda Coupland discovered when invited to join some friends intent on photographing gazelle. Her guide, a local gentleman, travelled with hooded falcon perched between the two front seats of his four-wheel drive vehicle which he skilfully navigated at around seventy miles per hour, across dunes, ditches and tracks apparently leading nowhere. The regally calm bird was about the only member of the group which appeared not to notice the jarring bumps of the rough desert tracks, throwing driver and passengers against the vehicle's ceiling. It was not long before an enthusiastic host proved that his route had been anything but aimless, for they halted in front of the only tree for miles around. This, he announced rather gravely, was the tree where the owls nest, as he jumped down to examine the ground around the tree, in search of gazelle droppings or tracks. Pointing to a flurry of apparently meaningless twisted tracks on the sand, he explained: "*snake tracks—made last night, see how the dew has formed upon them.*" and proceeded to examine what may or may not have been a hoofprint.

For four hours Linda's group tracked gazelle from the vehicle, sometimes stopping and searching the desert landscape for clues of the elusive creatures' hiding places; at other times peering down from the open windows of the vehicle, remarking upon signs of droppings pointed out to them by their indefatigable driver who continued

Arabian Sand Gazelle or Reem are native to the deserts of Arabia which they once inhabited in large numbers, forming huge herds, providing food for the region's inhabitants over thousands of years. Hunting was originally carried out by traditional methods but, since the introduction of the rifle and four-wheel drive vehicle, the local population has been severely depleted. (Furley)

Rugged scenery at Jebel Hafit, near Al Ain is the result of erosion of sedimentary rocks. (Vine)

to direct their attentions towards points of interest with one hand, while steering the vehicle at breakneck speed across corrugated bumps and gullies with the other. Their excitement to be finally brought within vision of wild gazelle is best communicated in Linda's own words. "*Suddenly, amongst the sparse scrub of a gravel-plain we discerned a movement. Lying up against the searing heat of the day, the gazelles had waited until the last moment before fleeing the oncoming vehicle, their tan coats blending in with the desert landscape. Three gazelles sprinted off with awe inspiring speed and grace, their powder-puff rumps flagging their course. We followed for a little while, recording a speed of* 65 *kilometres, managing to take a few photographs before falling back so as not to alarm the animals. We felt rewarded for our efforts but could not help reflecting that three gazelle in four hours of searching was a sad reflection on their depleted population.*"

Millions of years ago, before the rumblings of the Earth's crust separated the two, the huge landmass of Arabia formed part of a much larger continent, stretching from Asia to Africa, across which animals were able to migrate without hindrance by water barriers such as the Red Sea and Gulf which impede such an exchange today. Climatic changes associated with ice-ages and interglacial periods, wrought their own mark on the terrain giving rise, during the cooler period to vast forests and verdant plains carpeting Arabia, and when temperatures rose, to a collapse of these ecosystems and their replacement by arid zones or full-blown deserts . Arabia itself became virtually an island, bordered on three sides by sea, and across its northern borders by hostile desert. The territory of the Emirates, a small part of the peninsula, blessed with a remarkably wide range of scenery from majestic mountain ranges to a low coastal fertile belt, offered some respite and sanctuary from the relentless heat and persistent encroachment of the sands.

Over the course of time local species adapted to the particlar constraints of the environment, leading to a degree of subspeciation, and to the development of a characteristic fauna and flora. Desert sands of course predominated in the Emirates with the reknowned Empty Quarter, a 500,000 square kilometre sand-sea, butting on to the outskirts of Abu Dhabi itself. Despite the area's daunting hostility, for thousands of years bedouin tribesmen moved through the Empty Quarter and surrounding deserts, interpreting the language of nature, and adjusting their routes or camping schedules accordingly. Desert wildlife is capable of surviving for long periods without water. Some plants can remain dormant for many years, before springing back to life when a chance fall of rain moistens the soil. The Bedouin knew when to expect the rain, but it remained almost anyone's guess as to where it would fall. The 'desert telegraph' was however exceedingly efficient at passing the news among these nomadic herdsmen

The panoramic view from Jebel Hafit, near Al Ain, encompasses both an expanse of desert stretching out towards the Gulf coast, and the distant rising mountains of Oman. (Vine)

to whom one hour's rain could mean valuable pasturage for their camels and goats.

Now things have changed. The Emirates have drilled more wells and water supplies have become more accessible than before. There have been great strides in agriculture and the 'greening of the desert' is as impressive here as anywhere else in Arabia. Unfortunately the increased affluence and ability to grow crops has led to larger camel herds and flocks of goats and sheep, tending to throw things off balance again by leading to over-grazing problems and ultimate desertification, promoting encroachment of desert drifting sands on towns and villages once existing in closer harmony with their unique and strangely beautiful natural environment.

THE LANDSCAPE

The seven shaikhdoms comprising the UAE cover an area of approximately 78,000 square kilometres, forming a crescent of land towards the southern extremity of the Arabian peninsula, from Qatar to the northern border of Oman. Six of these shaikhdoms are on the west coast whilst Fujairah and some protectorates of Sharjah are situated on the eastern sea-board. This picture is further confused by the fact that several emirates possess inland enclaves, usually in the form of small oases, surrounded by a different emirate. The Hajar mountains, magnificent in their ruggedness, form a physical barrier between the northern emirates such as Ras Al Khaimah and the east coast.

Although both mountains and desert appear forbidding, archaeological excavations have unearthed evidence of settlements established here as early as several thousand years BC (see Chapter One). Despite the arrival of the 'modern age' and the considerable development of UAE's in-

A variety of sedges help to bind sand on coastal dunes, Jebel Ali. (Vine)

Pale sand dunes catch the evening light near the main road at Jebel Ali. (Vine)

frastructure through extensive road construction and urban development the wild landscape still dominates the Emirates, continually challenging Man's ingenuity or thwarting his efforts to tame nature.

UAE's coastline is dotted with limestone headlands, and sand banks, tidal flats, creeks and lagoons. Certain tidal locations have deposits of soft clays and carbonaceous silts, some of which are highly organic, inter-layered with denser gravels and sands. Coastal sand-dunes extend along most of the shore-line, formed by mixed carbonate sand made up of tiny particles of crushed shells. These carbonate dunes, larger in the south, commonly rest on a stable layer of carbonate and gypsum, underlain by solid limestone. Where a low coastal plain adjoins the shore-line, salt-flats or **sabkhas** occur and high evaporation rates concentrate salts as carbonates, sulphates and chlorides, rendering this one of the most hostile environments for plants and excluding all except a few algal species. Less severely saline habitats are colonised by a variety of halophytic species and many shallow lagoons or creeks support mangroves.

The width of the relatively level coastal-belt, sandwiched between the sea-shore on the one hand and rising hills on the other, varies from as little as one kilometre in northern Ras Al Khaimah to as much as two hundred kilometres in the southern area, near Abu Dhabi. Although the sandy desert zone forms about two thirds of the total area of the UAE, Abu Dhabi seems to have more than its fair share of this somewhat desolate terrain. The coastal zone between Abu Dhabi and Qatar has an extensive sandy area between the coastal **sabkhas** and inland dunes and along the Emirate's southern border lies the edge of the

The violently folded sedimentary rocks at Sha'am in Ras Al Khaimah bear silent witness to the tremendous upheaval which created this dramatic landscape from rocks formed under the sea. (Vine)

great Rub al Khali. Oases such as those at Liwa and Al Ain provide important refuges from this harsh desert environment and they have become havens where life flourishes and where local agriculture has blossomed to provide food for the entire region.

The contrast between well-planted streets and green fields within the oases and surrounding sand-dunes is remarkably strong. The dunes themselves tend to range in colour from white to cream along coastal areas, gradually becoming darker further inland, with those furthest from the coast taking on a rust red colour. This is due to the oxidising conditions of the arid climate, the sand grains often having a clay coating which oxidises to a rusty ferric iron metal. Typically, sand-dunes have abrupt ridges, sharpened by the wind. Some, known as 'Barchans', are asymmetrical crescent shaped dunes forming rows extending perpendicular to the prevailing wind-direction. Examples of these may be observed, aligned in a north-east to south-west pattern, between Al Ain and the Abu Dhabi coast. Dunes become larger as they stretch further inland, with some in the Empty Quarter as high as 250 metres. Wind whips across giant dune-tops, spraying fine films of sand into tranquil deserted valleys. Few places on earth evoke such timeless sensations of remoteness and of nature's wild, primitive power. The progress of such dunes (whose motion results from a continual process of accretion and degradation) across the landscape has been measured at a rate of around fifteen metres per year.

Towards the foot-hills, an elevated gravel plain divides coastlands from the mountains. Near the Hajar range surface soils comprise outwash materials, forming thick layers of gravel and boulders around the base of the mountains. The range itself, running approximately eighty kilometres, north-south, by thirty kilometres, east-west, and rising into peaks of 3,000 metres in Oman, is a formidable physical barrier and rain catchment feature. Formed by Jurassic and Cretaceous limestones and dolomites, together with basic igneous rocks, the mountains sustain very little vegetation, except along wadis. The latter, subject to periodic, devastatingly sudden flash-floods, are dissected by steep drainage channels running down to the gravel plains below. South of Fujairah the wadis run mainly eastwards, towards the sea, while to the north they flow westwards and into the sands.

Outwash deposits from wadi discharges help to fertilise local soils and in areas where underground water-supplies are tapped, productive agricultural projects have been established and natural vegetation flourishes. West of the Hajar range several fertile alluvial plains merge into a

Erosion has laid bare the geological story behind this dramatic landscape above the Acacia plain. (Furley)

Red sand-hills, coloured by oxidation of minerals (especially iron), stretch towards the Hajar mountain range and the border with Oman. Modern irrigation in this region has created many impressive agricultural projects. (Vine)

broader stony gravel plain, separating the mountains from the shifting dunes towards the coast. Along the east coast the mountains extend much closer to the shore-line and wadi deposits are mainly gravel and fine silt with soils generally poor in character, lacking nitrogen, potassium and phosphate.

CLIMATE

Climatological records from the UAE are available from the international airports at Abu Dhabi; Dubai; Sharjah; and Ras Al Khaimah, as well as from the Ministry of Agriculture and Fisheries' meteorological stations situated primarily in the northern Emirates. Aviation weather records commenced at Sharjah in 1932, in association with construction and operation of the Gulf's first civil airport. More recently, the opening of other airports and climatic recordings by government agencies, oil companies and experimental farms has considerably increased the data-base available for analysis.

Situated between 22 and 26 degrees north, the United Arab Emirates lies within a sub-region of the northern desert belt, characterised by scanty and erratic rainfall, and high levels for temperature, humidity, and sunshine. Winter sunshine averages eight hours per day whilst the summer figure reaches as high as eleven hours a day. Despite this apparently stable climatic picture, the weather does show a remarkable degree of local variability, throwing up thunderstorms, fog, gale force winds, sandstorms and, of course, rain. Average precipitation figures count for relatively little here since the range of readings, from one year to the next often exceeds twice the nominal 'average' figure , i.e. roughly 8 cms. (80mm.) per year. The Dubai Meteorological Office has annual records for rainfall ranging from 13.9mm to 202.7mm, and their results confirm that most rain falls in the winter months, from November to April. Less frequent, but nevertheless important rainfall occurs in isolated summer showers, carried into the area by south-westerly monsoons, and often occurring at the eastern edge of the great Rub al Khali, along the borders between Abu Dhabi and Saudi Arabia.

Summer months, from June to September are too hot for comfort, midday temperatures range from 35 degrees C. to 42 degrees C., and occasionally top 49 centigrade at the height of summer. During this period there is a sharp drop in night time temperatures, with these falling to roughly half the midday readings, i.e. 20 C. to 28 C, and providing a welcome respite from the searing heat of the day. Gulf waters exert a modifying influence on coastal zones which experience less dramatic diurnal fluctuations in temperature, and higher humidities than inland regions. Although the evenings are not so cool, coastal towns do have the advantage of pleasantly refreshing sea-breezes. Mountainous regions are also cooler and less hu-

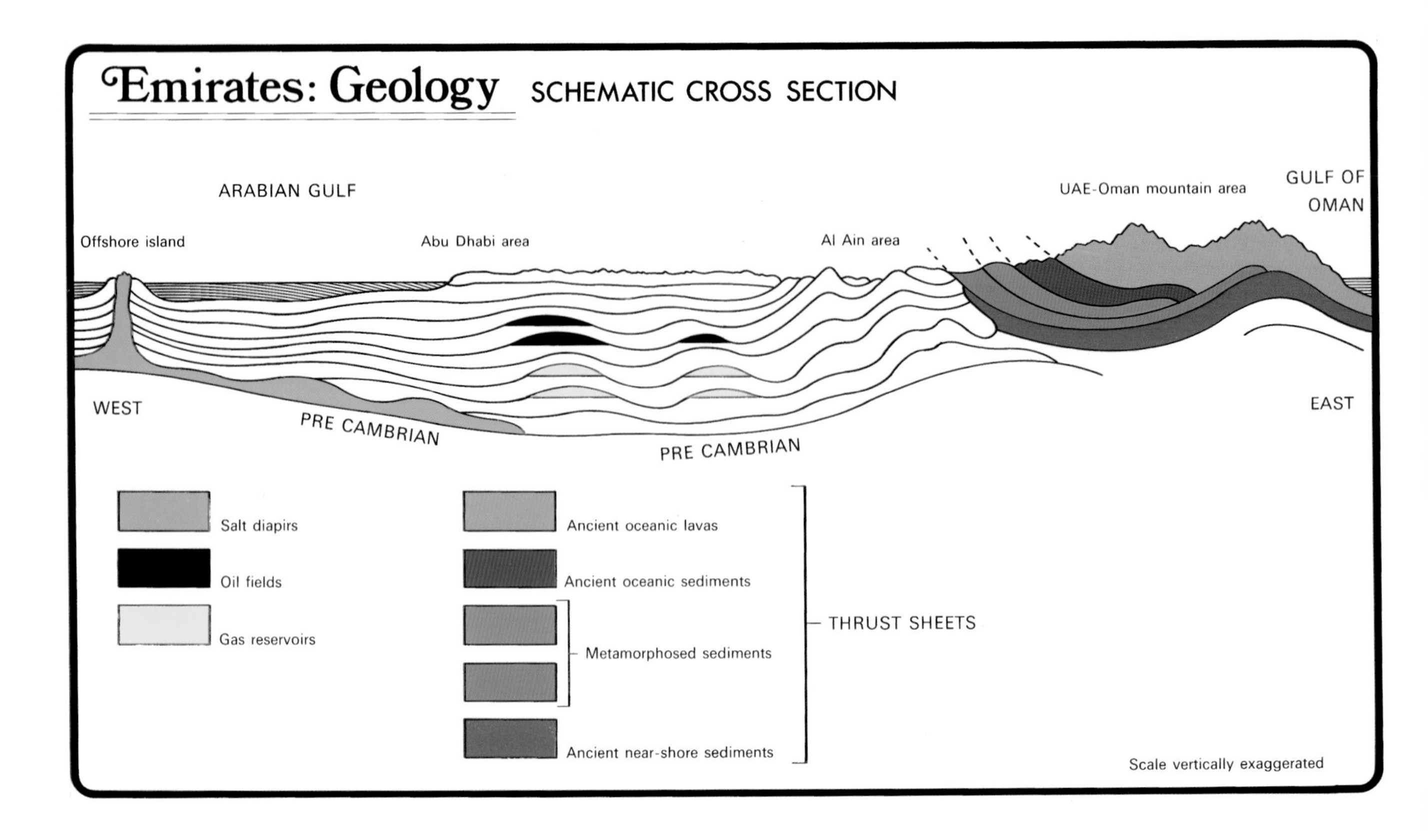

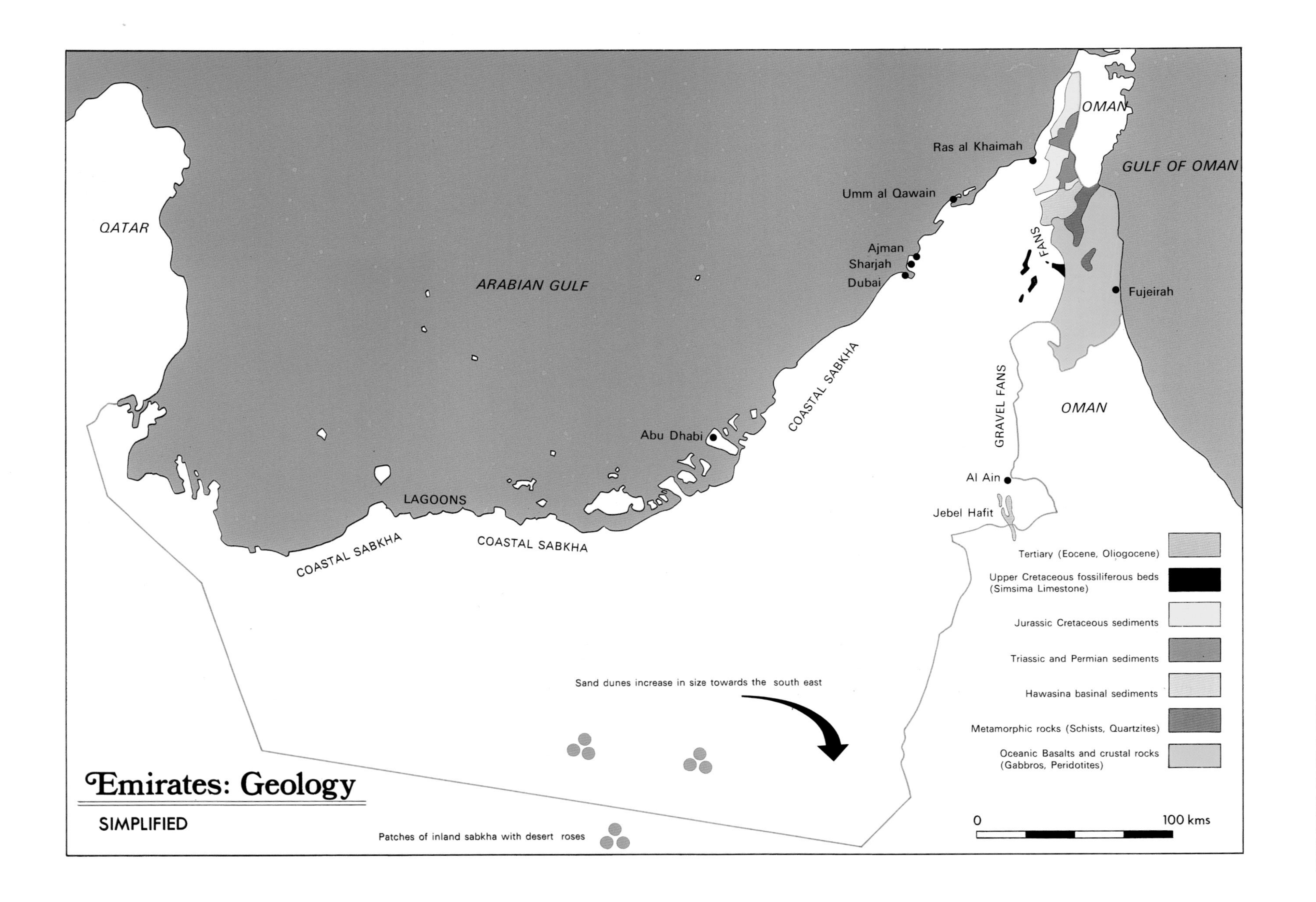
Emirates: Geology
SIMPLIFIED
QATAR
ARABIAN GULF
OMAN
GULF OF OMAN
Ras al Khaimah
Umm al Qawain
Ajman
Sharjah
Dubai
FANS
Fujeirah
COASTAL SABKHA
GRAVEL FANS
OMAN
Abu Dhabi
Al Ain
Jebel Hafit
LAGOONS
COASTAL SABKHA
COASTAL SABKHA
Tertiary (Eocene, Oliogocene)
Upper Cretaceous fossiliferous beds (Simsima Limestone)
Jurassic Cretaceous sediments
Triassic and Permian sediments
Hawasina basinal sediments
Metamorphic rocks (Schists, Quartzites)
Oceanic Basalts and crustal rocks (Gabbros, Peridotites)
Sand dunes increase in size towards the south east
Patches of inland sabkha with desert roses
0
100 kms

mid. From December to March, the climate is considerably more equable with midday temperatures ranging from 25 to 35 degrees Centigrade and falling to as low as 9 degrees at night.

The weather chart during much of the year shows a ridge of high pressure extending southwards into central Saudi Arabia with lower pressure over the eastern Gulf. Prevailing light to moderate north-westerly winds, known by their Arabic name **shamal**, meaning 'north', are associated with mid-latitude disturbances. Along the western coastal plain sea breezes tend to dominate with light south-south-easterlies at night being replaced by moderate north-westerlies during daytime. This pattern changes on the east coast where the proximity of the mountains results in gusty and less predictable wind shifts. A good strong blast of northerly **shamal** is usually preceeded in the UAE, by strong southerly winds, raising desert sands and reducing visibility. The shift to northerly winds may be quite sudden and can be accompanied by rain, thunderstorms, or duststorms. At sea, conditions can become quite difficult for small boats with force seven winds whipping up twelve foot high waves.

In summertime weather charts usually indicate a broad area of low pressure, extending from the western Sahara, across the Arabian peninsula and across Asia, to China. Local pressure variations in the Gulf combine with this to create weather conditions in the UAE. Steady north-westerlies, predominating in the central and northern regions of the Gulf, do not generally extend as far south as the UAE. When they do so, sea conditions around Abu Dhabi become quite rough, whilst the rest of UAE's coastal waters experience only slight swells.

Arabic interest in the weather and in the different types of winds blowing across the desert derives from the bedouin tribes for whom changes in weather could mean the difference between life and death. For them, each wind had its own characteristics and was known by a different name; thus the main period of storms was **Al-Barih al-owd** whilst the minor storm period was called **Al-Barih al-sagheer**. The first major **Shamal** occurring around May 25th is the **Al-Haffar**, or the "driller" since it drills huge depressions in the desert dunes. The second, arriving in early June, coincides with the dawn star, **Thorayya** (Pleiades) and is therefore named **Barih Thorayya**. During this one which is somewhat more violent than the others, fishermen tend to remain in port, not just because of the wind's strength, but because ancient folklore tells them that this wind devours ships! Near the end of June, the last shamal arrives; known as the **Al-Dabaran**, it is a violent wind, continuing for several days. Local residents keep doors and windows firmly barred in a battle against the all-penetrating fine dust driven by these **shamal** winds into every conceivable nook and cranny.

GEOLOGICAL FEATURES

While it is quite easy to picture the vast low coastal plains and desert of the UAE as once having been underwater, forming a shallow sea-bed, it is less easy to envisage the rugged peaks of Ras Al Khaimah as sharing similar origins, and yet one close look at their multi-layered twisted, crumbling structure reveals certain evidence of this. The ancient sea, once covering the whole region, rose and fell, influenced by major world climatic changes, and deposited its sediments for at least 500 million years. The layer of rocks thus formed is in places several kilometres thick and deep down, in air tight pockets of this ancient sea-bed, processes of decomposition have created oil and gas reserves providing the means for Man to transform the modern landscape. Earth movements folded and tilted these once horizontal layers during the mid-Tertiary; creating in the process scenic mountains such as Jebel Hafit and Jebel Huwayyah: a favourite place for studying evidence of this early marine period. The strange, fossil rich gorge, otherwise known as 'Fossil Valley' has been formed by erosion of an arched fold

Arthrocnemum macrostachy is a succulent halophytic plant usually found at water-logged sites, particularly along sheltered shore-lines of the UAE. (Western)

of sedimentary rocks. Cutting deep into the sedimentary series, erosion has exposed Upper Cretaceous ('Simsima') limestone; the remains of an offshore reef where corals , molluscs , echinoderms and other forms of sea-life once flourished. Here the amateur fossil hunter may encounter rock preserved samples of ancient marine-life, especially corals, rudists (oysters which look like corals) , clams, oysters, gastropods and even some ammonites. Similar finds may be made at Jebel Fa'Iyyah.

An interesting feature which observers sometimes find difficult to explain, is the existence of various rocks and minerals in the midst of a limestone series. These may consist of lavas, gypsum of various colours, haematite iron ore and mauve or green shales. Their origins are clearly separate from the biologically created limestone. The explanation lies in upsurges of salt deposits from beneath the limestone layers: extreme pressure on these, caused by overlying rocks, squeezes them up towards the surface through any weaknesses or cracks, dragging with them rocks from deep within the crust, sometimes from 6,000 metres down. When the salt rock pierces the surface it is quite rapidly eroded, depositing the boulders and debris it has brought up with it. Current examples of this phenomenon may be seen at Jebel Dhanna, Sir Bani Yas, Das, Zirku and on several other islands.

Unlike the Asir mountains along the Red Sea coast of Saudi Arabia and Yemen, which have dominated the landscape for hundreds of millions of years, the Hajar range is a relatively recent phenomenon, only 15 to 20 million years old. It is a geologically distinct feature, separate from the sabkhas, desert and low jebels discussed above. From a geologist's viewpoint these tall mountains, forming a natural boundary between Oman and UAE, are of great interest since they offer a relatively rare opportunity to examine oceanic rocks, such as basalts, lavas and oozes, formed at the site of a mid-oceanic ridge more than seventy million years ago. During the Cretaceous period the movement of oceanic plates resulted in this segment of the earth's crust being dragged towards Arabia and eventually being pushed onto the edge of the peninsula. Great pressures were clearly involved in the process, altering crustal rocks and lavas into green-grey ophiolites and dark brown gabbros which we see today on the majestic craggy peaks south of Dibba and Misafi. At first this movement did not necessarily entail uplift of the oceanic rocks above sea-level, and they did in fact form a new sea-bed on top of which other sediments were deposited. This may be observed from the road to Hatta, and through Jebel Fa'Iyyah, where Upper Cretaceous limestones are resting on top of an older sea-bed of lavas.

Today's scenery is primarily a relic of the Ice Age during which a much wetter climate resulted in large rivers tearing down the mountains, cutting into their sides, and carrying vast quantities of gravel, pebbles and boulders which were washed out , forming huge alluvial fans, filling-up the valleys and extending on to the surrounding plains. Since then, sun and wind have continued to weather rock surfaces while flash-floods can still result in alluvial deposits.

PLANT LIFE

Natural vegetation of the UAE is dominated by arid zone species, many of which can survive for long periods without water. Plant-life varies according to local conditions, and in the following discussion very broad habitat classifications have been selected, while only dominant species are discussed.

1. Coastal Vegetation

Coastal areas where the substrate is either mud or sand, occasionally with a thin covering of topsoil, provide habitats for a number of species including the beach grass *Halopyrum mucrunatum*, salt-marsh plants such as *Arthrocnemum glaucum*, together with a variety of rushes, reeds and sedges.

Halopeplis perfoliata, primarily a coastal succulent plant, is tolerant of salt, and relatively common along the shore-line. (Western)

The mangrove, *Avicennia marina*, has suffered greatly from various land-reclamation projects here, as elsewhere along the entire Arabian coastline. Several major stands of mangroves still occur in the UAE however and protection orders have been placed on some of these. (Western)

Along certain sheltered areas of coastline the mangrove, *Avicennia marina* forms quite dense fringing thickets of greenery, especially in Ras Al Khaimah, in the Abu Dhabi area, and at Khor Kalba on the east coast, in Fujairah.

Salt-flats or sabkhas, comprising aeolian or mixed calcareous sand, may harbour plants with spreading root systems, able to absorb moisture close to the surface. *Salicornia* sp. (Glasswort) is an example of such a salt-tolerant plant and is presently being grown as a forage crop at Kalba. Where mud gives way to mixed calcium carbonate and stony deposits other halophytic plants, grasses and the parasitic *Cistanche* occur. Salt content in the semi-arid zones can reach anything up to 23,000 parts per million, naturally decreasing further inland, with levels down to around 12,500 parts per million 22 kms from the coast. Such conditions challenge all but the hardiest of species. In some areas, i.e. the true sabkhas, even these are eliminated since crusts of gypsum, anhydrite and calcite prevent virtually everything except algae from growing.

Along the coastline between Abu Dhabi and Qatar, highly saline sabkhas extend over a large area of the coastal plain but further north, from Abu Dhabi towards Dubai, the coastline is slighly more elevated and several halophytic bushes begin to appear, including the bright green common *Zygophyllum* sp., *Halopeplis perfoliata* with red and orange fleshy leaves, and *Haloxylon salicornicum*. The flowering Sea Lavender, *Limonium axillare*, also occurs here, with its purple flowers, opening in February and March, introducing new colour to the coastal tract, together with numerous insects.

2. Semi-desert Areas

In those areas where conditions are not so completely arid as the true desert, a number of trees and plants occur. A typical member of this habitat is the thorny, flat-topped tree, *Acacia tortilis*, which flowers in June and July and has long tap roots capable of penetrating many metres underground, reaching the hidden water table. Another tree with long tap roots is the Ghaf, *Prosopis spicigera*, which survives in areas where no rainfall

Limonium axillare has bright purple flowers and generally occurs where water is retained among rocks or in shallow depressions. (Western)

North of Hili, on the Al Ain to Dubai main road, the route travels along the border of an Acacia plain, irrigated by run-off from the Hajar range of mountains. Many large farms have been established in this area, taking advantage of a good supply of ground-water. (Vine)

occurs for as long as five years. Its bright yellow, catkin-like flowers blossom in March and April. Apart from an extensive root system, it is also able to absorb water through its leaves, a fact which no doubt encourages grazing by camels. This tree is greatly valued by Bedouin as a source of fire-wood and, in consequence, its distribution has been quite severely curtailed.

Calligonum comosum, locally known as Arta, is a well adapted perennial which retains its essential moisture during drought periods in fleshy roots, remaining dormant until rain appears. At most times this plant, with its twisted and broken stems, appears to be dead or withered. In February and March however it produces small white fruits with reddish tufts along the outer twigs.

A road-side sign warns of the danger of flash-floods filling the Wadi after heavy rains, leaving a broad expanse of alluvial gravel. In the distance an Acacia plain stretches towards the foothills. (Vine)

Succulents, such as the Euphorbias, are able to close their stomata during the hottest part of the day, thus avoiding moisture loss through transpiration. *Euphorbia larica*, or Isbaq, has such small leaves (a clear adaptation to arid conditions) that its stem has adopted a photosynthetic function.

3. Inland deserts

The vast open deserts of southern Arabia appear to be hostile to all plants; those that survive among the shifting sand dunes and arid plains are some of the most fascinating of species, displaying unique adaptations for retention of their essential water balance.

The Little Rose of Jericho (*Anastatica hierochuntica*) is one which intrigues botanists by its ability to roll into a very tight ball until a shower of rain causes it to suddenly unfold, revealing green leaf rosettes surrounding small flowers. It is a hygrochastic species, storing seeds for a year before releasing them at the optimum period for their development. Several sedges survive among the desert sand-dunes of the Emirates, in particular, *Cyperus conglomeratus* and *Dipterygium glaucum*. In the Liwa area the "Markh" bush (*Leptadenia pyrotechnica*) is encouraged as a means of stabilising sand-dunes. In March it displays masses of small yellow flowers and from a distance superficially resembles a large patch of marram grass.

Whilst the majority of desert plants are wind

Dipterigium glaucum. (Western)

The "Easter Palm", *Calligonum comosum*, is a true desert plant, utilised by the Bedu for thousands of years for a variety of purposes. The wood of this versatile bush was used for burning; the fruits as a source of nourishment; and its crushed dried leaves formed a treatment for skin ailments. (Western)

pollinated, some do depend on attracting insects to their flowers in order to effect pollination. In some cases such species open their flowers only in the early morning and evening, closing during the heat of the day. This occurs for example with Capers whose cucumber like fruits are a distinctive identifying feature.

Many of the desert plants are potentially vulnerable to grazing by camels, and several have adaptive features which discourage this. Senna, *Cassia italica*, causes diarrhoea, as do several *Zygophyllum* species, including *Z.hamiense*. The latter has bright green succulent leaves and small white flowers arising between leaf and branchlet joints. Two other desert plants generally avoided by herbivores are Harmal or poisonous *Rhazya stricta* (a member of the Oleander family usually found on gravel plains rather than on sand) and Ushar, (*Calotropis procera*) commonly known as the Gunpowder tree. When cut or damaged this species exudes a poisonous white liquid. Whatever about its ability to ward off possible grazers, it does an excellent job of attracting small bees and wasps to its dense green leaves and small white five-petalled, mauve bordered flowers.

The Red Thumb, *Cynomorium coccineum* is a parasitic plant, dark reddish brown with a long fleshy stalk and bulbous head. The stem reaches far down under the sand and attaches itself to its host plant by means of a thin strand. The Desert Hyacinth (*Cistanche tubulosa*) has a yellow hyacinth shaped flower and inhabits both desert and coastal areas.

The biochemical properties of various desert plants have been known to the Bedu for thousands of years. While some plants are used in medicines, others are treasured for dyes or cosmetics, while still more may have edible roots or be favoured for firewood. Rak, *Salvadora persica*, provides desert dwellers with the equivalent of a toothbrush or **miswak**. There is undoubtedly still a great deal to be learned from local knowledge of desert plants and several institutions in Arabia are carrying out research in this interesting field.

The desert hyacinth, *Cistanche tubulasa*, is a parasitic plant, depending on growth of its host, the goosefoot (*Chenopodiaceae*). Seeds of the hyacinth may remain dormant for many years, until rain stimulates development of the goosefoot which in turn triggers germination of the hyacinth. Despite its name, this plant is remarkably widespread, usually occurring in wadis but also along the coastline of the UAE. (Western)

Silene villosa. (Western)

4. Plant-life of Wadis

Wadis, or dried river beds, harbour many perennial plants. Fourteen carnation species (*Caryophyllaceae*) have been recorded from wadis in the UAE. The Oleanders, *Nerium oleander* and *Nerium mascatense* form attractive flowering bushes, mainly in mountain wadis towards the north-east. Falaj irrigated wadis shelter ferns, lavenders and orchids. In a few wadis the Maidenhair fern, *Adiantum capillus veneris* can be found growing in association with the orchid *Epipactis veratrifolia*, forming a rare floral community in the Arabian peninsula.

Lodged between the rocky wadi substrata one may encounter the purple flowering *Tephrosia* and the evergreen shrub *Pulicaria glutinosa*, the latter reaching a height of 70 cms. Jebel Hafit, with its extensive gravel plains, mountain terraces and boulder filled wadis, harbours a number of interesting species including *Ochradenus aucheri*, a woody perennial with spiny branches and spiky yellow flowers preceding the appearance of fleshy yellow berries. Another species found here is *Zilla spinosa*, a spiny perennial with lilac blooms and warty tapered green fruits.

The Isbaq or *Euphorbia tirucalli*, a candelabra shaped leafless succulent, may grow as high as a metre and a half in wadis, whilst the annual herb *Chrozophora verbascifolia*, reaches similar dimensions.

Ochradenus baccatus is usually found among the stony foot-hills of the UAE. It flowers in winter and its small leaves are an adaptation to minimise water-loss. (Western).

Spring-time ephemerals found in wadis include several small flowers, only a few inches in height, which nestle between rocks, such as *Indigofera arabica* (silver green with red flowers), *Hippocrepis constricta* (possessing strangely contorted seed pods), and *Argyrobolium roseum* (with trifoliate leaves and small pinkish flowers).

5. Plant-life of Northern Emirates and East Coast

Ras Al Khaimah is one of the most fertile areas of the Emirates, with its relatively narrow coastal plain sandwiched between rugged high mountains and the Arabian Gulf. The precipitous mountain sides, plunging wadis and sheer cliff-faces provide an abundance of habitats for small wild plants. Ferns, such as *Onychium divaricatum*, with fronds over 20 cms long, are relatively abundant. Larger perennials like *Dyerophytum indicum* with its pro-

Nerium mascatense. (Western)

Astragalus fasciculifolis. (Western)

fuse orange-yellow flowers and thin wands of the deep purple flowering *Periploca aphylla* occur in wadis near Ras Al Khaimah, often in association with the bush *Pulicaria glutinose*. Hidden among the boulders and rock faces of the seemingly uninhabited mountain-sides, the alert observer will notice remains of stone houses, perched on narrow terraces, commanding strategic views of the surrounding countryside. Many of these have been recently abandoned in favour of the modern dwellings the emirate is now able to offer its people. It was in the protected compound of one such house that botanists in 1985 found the rare Iris, *Iris sisyrinchium* living in association with *Medicago polymorpha* and *Heterocaryum szovitsianum*.

The east coast of the UAE, extending as it does from Dibba in the north to Khor Kalba in the south, consists of a relatively narrow plain, approximately six kilometers wide in the south, narrowing towards Dibba which is at the foothills of the Oman mountains. The date palm, *Phoenix dactylifera*, grows right down to the shoreline, indicating that sea-water seepage has not infiltrated the fresh-water table. Along the sea-shore, especially in sheltered regions, mangroves are abundant and Khor Kalba presented a unique coastal habitat prior to the encroachment of urban development. Growing among the pebbles above the main tidal channel flowing into the harbour of Khor Kalba one will find the pink *Polycarpea spicata*.

Mangifera indica. (Western)

Dodonea viscosa. (Western)

The Date Palm

Date palms have been valued and fully exploited by local people for thousands of years. Apart from the nutritious fruit, highly suitable for preservation and storage, virtually every other part of the tree had a particular use. Leaves, fronds, fibres and trunk were used for fencing, roofing, weaving, rope-making, boat-building and as a general housing material. Trunks could be attached to fishing nets to help keep them buoyant and **shashahs** or small fishing boats were made from cane and palm leaves. Ropes of varying thicknesses and lengths served for tethering livestock, fishing and for mooring their boats; anything left over was burnt for firewood. The date palm has held a special place in the Arab heart since time immemorial. There is an old saying: "dates are the fertilizers of our knees, they give us strength and energy".

Arabian sweets and pastries such as **shabal** rely heavily on dates and they are also used in jams and syrups. Dates are the traditional accompaniment of coffee and were a favourite source of energy for pearl divers with the crew of a single pearling vessel frequently requiring 100 kilograms of dates per day.

Fujairah and Ras Al Khaimah are the major date producers in the UAE and eighty percent of available fruit growing land is occupied by date palm plantations. Clusters of dates, often three feet long and more than a foot in diameter hang from many of the trees and, in 1986 alone, Ras Al Khaimah produced 20,000 tonnes of dates. A wide range of varieties are cultivated in the UAE, with the yellow Nighal, Fardh and Bagal fairly common although not as high in quality as the red varieties of Khinaizy, Khisab and Muselli more suitable for fresh consumption than the yellow forms which are usually dried.

Date palms, *Phoenix dactylifera* at Sha'am, Ras Al Khaimah. (Western)

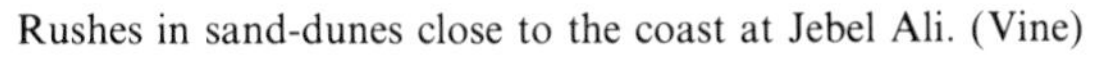

Rushes in sand-dunes close to the coast at Jebel Ali. (Vine)

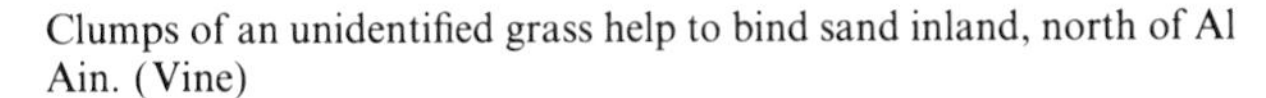

Clumps of an unidentified grass help to bind sand inland, north of Al Ain. (Vine)

LIST OF COMMON TREES, SHRUBS AND PLANTS FOUND IN THE UAE*

Family	Species	Habitat
ADIANTACEAE	*Adiantum capillusveneris*	Wet soil
AIZOACEAE	*Aizoon canariense*	Salty/Sandy
AMARANTHEEAE	*Aerva javanica*	Sandy soil
ANACARDIACEAE	*Mangifera indica* (Mango)	Plantations/wadis
APOCYANAEAE	*Nerium mascatense* (native Oleander)	Plantations/wadis
	Nerium oleander (Mediterranean Oleander)	Plantations/wadis
	Plumeria acutifolia (Frangipani)	Plantations/wadis
	Rhazya stricta	Gravel plains
ASCLEPIADACEAE	*Calotropis procera* (Sodom apple)	Sandy soil
	Leptadenia pyrotechnica	Sand dunes
	Periploca apylla	Mountains
BORAGINACEAE	*Cordia sebestena* (Scarlet cordia)	Plantations
	Moltkiopsis ciliata	Sandy soil
	Arnebia hispidissima	Sandy soil
	Heliotropium kotschyi	Salty soil
CACTACEAE	*Opuntia engelmannii* (Prickly pear)	Sandy soil
CAPPARACEAE	*Capparis cartilaginea*	Mountains
	Capparis spinosa	Plantations
	Dipterygium glaucum	Sandy soil
CARYOPHYLLACEAE	*Cometes surattensis*	Rocky hills/plains
	Polycarpaea spicata	Sandy soil
	Sclerocephalus arabicus	Sandy/rocky areas
	Silene villosa	Sand dunes
	Saponaria barbata	Sandy soil
CASUARINACEAE	*Casuarina equisetifolia* (Whispering Pine)	Plantations/ Shelter belt.
EUPHORBIACEAE	*Euphorbia arabica*	Rocky hills
	Euphorbia hirta	Rocky hills
	Euphorbia larica	Rocky hills
	Ricinus communis (Castor oil plant)	Plantations
GENTIANACEAE	*Centaurium pulchellum*	Wet wadi
GERANIACEAE	*Erodium malacoides*	Sandy soil
	Erodium neuradifolium	Sandy soil
	Geranium mascatense	Wadi
GRAMINAE	*Cenchrus ciliaris*	Sandy soil
	Halopyrum mucronatum	Sandy soil
	Sporobolos spicatus	Sandy soil

CHENOPODIACEAE	*Arthrocnemum macrostachyum*	Marsh/salty soil
	Cornulaca monocantha	Sandy soil
	Halopeplis perfoliata	Salty/sandy soil
	Hammada elegans	Sandy soil
	Salsola baryosma	Salty soil
	Salsola schweinfurthii	Sandy soil
COMBRETACEAE	*Terminalia catappa* (Indian Almond)	Plantations
COMPOSITAE	*Launea capitata*	Sandy soil
	Reichardia tingitana	Sand/gravel
CONVOLVULACEAE	*Convolvulus prostratus*	Rocky areas
	Ipomea biloba (Goat's foot)	Sandy soil
CRUCIFERAE	*Anasthatica hierochuntica*	Gravel plains/hills
	Diplotaxis harra	Rocky plains
	Eremobium aegyptiacum	Sandy soil
	Erucaria hispanica	Sandy soil
	Physorrhyncus chaemarapistum	Rocky plain
	Savignya parviflora	Sandy soil
	Zilla spinosa	Sandy/rocky areas
CYPERACEAE	*Cyperus conglomeratus*	Sandy soil
LABIATAE	*Salvia macilanta*	Rocky/wadis
LEGUMINOSAE	*Acacia arabica* (Arabic Gum tree)	Plantations, Sandy soil
	A. auriliculiformis	Rocky/sandy areas
	A. decurrens (Green wattle)	Plantations
	A. ehrenbergiana	Sandy soil
	A. tortilis	Gravel/plantations
	Albizzia lebbeck (Fry wood tree)	Plantations
	Argyrolobium roseum	Gravel plains
	Astragalus fasciculifolius	Mountains
	Cassia italica	Sandy soil/wadis
	Indigofera arabica	Rocky plains/wadis
	Caesalpinea bonduc (Indian nut)	Plantations
	Melilotus indica	Sandy/plantations
	Lotus halophilus	Salty soil
	Parkinsonia aculeata (Jerusalem thorn)	Plantations
	Peltophorum inerme (Rusty shieldbearer)	Plantations
	Pongamia glabra (Pongam)	Plantations
	Prosopis juliflora (Mesquite)	Plantations
	P. spicigera	Sand dunes
LILIACEAE	*Aloe vera*	Plantations
	Asphodelus fistulosus	Sand/gravel

(Note:- Plantations include city gardens, parks etc). * This list is based on one prepared by members of the UAE Natural History Society.

LYTHRACEAE	*Lawsonia inermis* (Henna)	Plantations
MALVACEAE	*Hibiscus rosa sinensis* (Chinese shoe flower)	Plantations
	Malva aegyptiaca	Sandy soil
	Malvaviscus arboreus (Turks Hat Hibiscus)	Plantations
	Thespesia populaea (Aden apple)	Plantations
MORACEAE	*Ficus benghalensis* (Banyan)	Plantations
	F. carica (Common Fig)	Mountains/wadis
	F. nitida (Laurel fig)	Wadis/ Mountains
	Morus nigra (Mulberry)	Mts/Plantations
MORINGACEAE	*Moringa oleifera* (Drumstick tree)	Plantations
MYRTACEAE	*Callestemon speciosus* (Australian bottle brush)	Plantations
	Eucalyptus camaldulensis (Red gum)	Plantations, Shelter belts
	Melaleuca leucadendron	Plantations
NYCTAGINACEAE	*Boerhaavia elegans*	Rocky areas
	Bougainvillea glabra	Plantations
	B. spectabilis	Plantations
OLEACEAE	*Jasminum sambac* (Arabian jasmine)	Plantations
	Olea europaea (Olive tree)	Sandy soil
ORCHIDACEAE	*Epipactis veratrifolia*	Plantations
OROBANCHACEAE	*Cistanche tubulosa*	Sandy/salty soil
PALMACEAE	*Cocos nucifera* (Coconut palm)	Plantations
	Phoenix dactylifera (Date palm)	Plantations
	Washingtonia robusta (Californian fan palm)	Plantations
PLANTAGINACEAE	*Plantago afra*	Sandy soil
	P. ovata	Sandy soil
PLUMBAGINACEAE	*Dyerophytum indicum*	Wadis
	Limonium axillare (Sea Lavender)	Salty soil
	Plumbago capensis (Leadwort)	Sandy soil
POLYGONACEAE	*Antigonon leptopus* (Coral vine)	Sandy soil
	Calligonum comosum	Sandy soil
	Rumex vesicarius	Rocky plains
PORTULACACEAE	*Portulaca grandiflora*	Sandy soil
	P. olereaca	Sandy soil

PRIMULACEAE	*Anagallis arvensis*	Plantations
RHAMNACEAE	*Ziziphus jujuba* (Chinese date)	Plantations
	Z. spina-christi (Crown of Thorns)	Plantations
RHIZOPHORACEAE	*Avicennia marina* (Grey mangrove)	Marsh/coastal
SALVADORACEAE	*Salvadora persica* (Rak bush)	Low mountains
SAPINDACEAE	*Dodoea viscosa*	Plantations
SCROPHULARIACAE	*Schweinfurthia papillionacea*	Wadi/coastal
	Scrophularia deserti	Rocky plains
SOLANACEAE	*Lycium shawii*	Low mountains
	Solanum nigrum	Plantations
TAMARICACEAE	*Tamarix aphylla*	Salty soil
	T. articulata	Salty soil
	T. passerinoides	Salty soil
VERBENACEAE	*Clerodendron inerme* (Wild jasmine)	Plantations
	Lantana camara (Common lantana)	Mts/Plantations
	Lippia nodiflora	Plantations
VITACEAE	*Vitis vinifera* (Grape vine)	Plantations
ZYGOPHYLLACEAE	*Fagonia indica*	Rocky plains
	Tribulus omanense	Sandy soil
	Tribulus terrestris	Sandy soil
	Zygophyllum hamiense	Salty soil
	Zygophyllum simplex	Sandy soil

MARINE LIFE

Bordered on one side by the neritic seas of the Indian Ocean, and on the other by the more saline and enclosed waters of the Gulf, the Emirates offer the marine enthusiast the best of both worlds. The Arabian Gulf is itself a relatively young sea, being formed roughly four million years ago. Since its inception as a broad shallow basin, changes in sea-level associated with glacial and interglacial periods have resulted in successive drownings and emersions of the Gulf's surface; alternately giving rise to a shallow sea or a low swampy area of fertile land through which the huge estuary of the Euphrates river once wended it way. Roughly twenty thousand years ago sea-level again rose, as the world entered its most recent interglacial period, and by five thousand years ago the present day sea-level was achieved. There have been further minor fluctuations since then, but the above summary does emphasise the relatively brief history of the Gulf as we know it.

This great shallow body of water (average depth 35m.), the focus of so much world attention, is approximately 1,000 kms long and two to three hundred kms wide, and by virtue of the constricted entrance to the Indian Ocean, via the Straits of Hormuz, it is virtually land-locked. Its maximum depth of 100m. occurs along the coast of Iran and restricted water exchange, together with high evaporation rates cause higher salinity levels than in the Indian Ocean.

Water exchange via the sixty kms wide bottleneck at Hormuz takes place at two levels, with

The Thrush Cowrie, *Cypraea turdus*, in shallow-water off the coast of Ras Al Khaimah. (Woodward)

Typical view of a Textile Cone taken at Sharma Rocks in about six metres. (Woodward)

lighter Indian Ocean waters flowing in from the Gulf of Oman at the surface, compensated by an outflow of heavier, more saline water. Waters thus flowing in to the Gulf provide important nutrient replenishment, and help to moderate salinity levels somewhat. The northern end of the Gulf, near the Tigris-Euphrates-Karun delta, or Shatt-al Arab, is less saline as a result of the river flowing into the Gulf, carrying with it terrigenous deposits. Generally, as one moves south, salinity levels rise so that some coastal lagoons have levels as high as seventy parts per thousand and, along the western coast of the UAE, where there are no inflowing rivers to dilute the sea, levels are notoriously high, ranging from 42ppt offshore to 67ppt at inner lagoons. Sea temperatures at the surface vary throughout the Gulf with UAE coastal waters dropping as low as 10 deg.C. in winter contrasting sharply with 35 deg.C. summer temperatures. Offshore, sea-temperatures experience a somewhat less dramatic seasonal range, generally between winter minimum of 15 deg. C. and a summer maximum of 33 deg. C. One result of the Gulf's shallow nature is that sea-surface temperatures affect the entire water column, unlike oceanic waters where the great body of deep sea water acts as a buffer, moderating seasonal climatic effects.

Tidal currents along the west coast are relatively slow, at 0.3m/sec. with tidal range varying within the Gulf from 4.0m in the north, to less than a metre in the south. At times of high spring tides in the Gulf of Oman, waters gush into the Gulf much faster, with speeds reaching 0.7m/sec but there is such a delaying effect that these waters do not extend far before the falling tide outside causes a current reversal and a consequent outflow of these rich and productive waters.

The extreme physical parameters of the marine environment in the Arabian Gulf restrict the number of species occuring there, and in areas where salinities or temperatures reach unusually high (or low) levels, even Gulf species themselves may be unable to survive. The rather unique conditions pertaining here, together with the relative isolation of the Gulf from other major water-bodies, has resulted in quite a high level of endemism among those forms which do occur. Waters off the east coast of the UAE are quite different in character, being essentially oceanic and thus less saline and experiencing much smaller annual fluctuations in temperature. Here, coastal reefs may be more developed and harbour a greater variety of sea-life.

COASTAL SHALLOWS AND INTERTIDAL FLATS

Along the Gulf coast of the Emirates are numerous low sandy islands, small bays and shallow lagoons which are significant features in the survival of numerous marine species. Here, protected from strong waves, sands and muds accumulate, seagrasses flourish, providing valuable nurseries for commercially important shrimps and fish. Intertidal mud-flats, sloping at an average of 35cm vertical height per kilometre, may themselves be several kilometres broad at low-tide, and provide a rich habitat for numerous burrowing organisms.

BEACHES

Sandy beaches are formed from carbonate sand mixed with minute fragments of crushed shells and corals together with some quartz grains washed or blown off the desert. While the intertidal level of the beach is sculpted into a pattern of parallel corrugations, higher up there is a series of tide- marks where flotsam and jetsam have accumulated, and above that a barrier of sand dunes anchored in place by beach grasses and other plants.

The beach itself is a fascinating place to search for the myriad life-forms which exist here. Rocks, generally of sandstone, limestone or siltstone, provide valuable anchoring points for numerous sedentary creatures. Towards the upper level of the beach, just above tide level, one may see many Ghost Crabs, *Ocypode saratan*. These are probably best observed at night-time scurrying along the beach, off-white carapaces and long stalked eyes rendering their common name entirely justified. Ghost Crabs are general scavengers feeding on almost anything offered, but frequently hunting other shore crabs such as Mole Crabs and Mud Crabs which they have been seen digging out of their burrows: they also eat young turtle hatchlings. Male Ghost Crabs build pyramid-like sand towers, up to 30 cms. high, alongside their burrows, signalling their presence to both Man and fellow crabs.

SEAGRASS BEDS

Seagrass beds are really like underwater meadows providing a rich food source for dugongs, turtles, and many fish and invertebrates. More than five hundred species have been identified in association with sea-grass beds in the Arabian Gulf, and apart from providing food, they are important refuges for juveniles of many fish. Three species of sea-grasses commonly occur in the Gulf; i.e. *Halodule uninervis*; *Halophila ovalis* and *Halophila stipulacea*, all tolerant to high salinity and turbidity such as occur along the UAE coastline. *Halodule uninervis* has long thin grass-like blades, approximately 3mm wide and 25 cms long.

Portrait of a Stonefish taken at Dibba Island, Fujairah. This potentially lethal fish was found on sand under a coral overhang. (Woodward)

H. stipulacea may be found mixed with *H. uninervis* from which it is clearly distinguishable by virtue of its somewhat mint-like leaves, about 10cms long. *H. ovalis*, as its name suggests, has small oval leaves born on a narrow stem. All three species bury their spreading roots in the sediment. It is impossible to over-emphasise the important role of these underwater meadows in the future well-being of marine-life since they play a vital function in supporting local fisheries as well as providing essential food for endangered species.

CORAL REEFS AND CORALS

The Arabian Gulf is a relatively stressful environment for many corals. Reef-building species were, until recently, believed not to occur where winter temperatures fall below 20 deg. C. In the Gulf this is plainly not the case since coral-reefs, comprised it must be admitted of a limited number of species, exist in places where winter lows of only 10 deg. C, have been recorded! In this sense at least, Arabian Gulf coral-reefs are particularly interesting to scientists. An additional factor affecting coral-growth in the Gulf is the high level of local turbidity and the associated clogging affect of fine silt.

Among the fifty or so coral species, belonging to twenty-four genera, which inhabit the Arabian Gulf, perhaps the most important reef-builders are Acroporas such as *Acropora humilis* while the meandrine *Leptoria* and smooth rounded star-coral, *Porites* are also important. The latter genus forms large boulder-like colonies up to three metres in diameter. Corals such as these build reefs which provide habitats for fascinating communities of fish, crabs, sea-urchins, anemones, crustaceans, molluscs, echinoderms and many other organisms.

Blenny at Jumeira, Dubai, 5 metres. (Woodward)

Hovering in the water, never venturing far from the protective refuge of the reef, are numerous brightly coloured and gaily patterned fish whose behaviour is particularly adapted to survive in this environment. Apart from shoaling, which has considerable survival value for individuals within a group, there are numerous other strategies employed by locally occurring reef-fish. One, which frequently draws comments from divers, is that of the exaggeratedly aggressive yet hopelessly small damselfish. It would seem quite impossible for a two inch long fish, lacking any of nature's defensive armaments such as a venomous bite, poisonous spines or razor sharp 'scalpels', to actually frighten a fully grown, shark seeking scuba diver; and yet this happens. Damselfish, members of the family *Pomacentridae*, come in a variety of forms including the Three-spot Damselfish (*Dascyllus trimaculatus*), Sergeant- majors (*Abudefduf saxatilis vaigiensis*), and Clown-fish (*Amphiprion*) which choose to live among the tentacles of giant sea-anemones. While each of these may show a certain degree of aggression in defending their own patch of reef, few can equal the pugnacious dull coloured *Stegastes nigricans* damselfish for sheer guts in the face of apparently impossible odds. This 'dark horse' literally bluffs it out against all intruders, however large they may be. Divers who persist in remaining within their territory are likely to be bombarded by a host of very angry fish, and are left in no doubt that their presence is an unwelcome intrusion upon their right to privacy. Although the damselfish are unable to harm a diver, they nevertheless succeed in unnerving all but the most hard-hearted and insensitive.

Anemone fish are also a source of great interest to divers since they are relatively unafraid and can be easily approached. If one persists in aggravating them, they retreat among their host anemone's stinging tentacles, quite oblivious to the potentially lethal batteries of stinging cells. This immunity apparently results from the clown-fish coating its own body with a thin film of mucus secreted by the anemone: just as the anemone does not sting itself, so the mucus coat imparts protection to the anemone-fish.

For the SCUBA diver and snorkeller, the UAE offers many fascinating experiences underwater with a variety of habitats to be explored, ranging from coral-reefs to old wrecks. The reefs themselves abound with exquisite and gaily patterned fish sharing their habitat with other colourful oc-

Pink colonies of the soft coral *Dendronephthya* adorn the reef-face at ten metres depth on 'Martini Rock', Khor Fakkan. (Dipper)

cupants such as anemones, sponges, crabs, molluscs and echinoderms, together with many territorial reef-fish. Pelagic, or open water fish, patrol the reef-edge, hunting unwary prey, or perhaps sieving plankton. The presence of numerous wrecks has in effect greatly increased the amount of locally present "reef-life" since these have provided hard surfaces for attachment of corals and other invertebrates as well as instantly available nooks and crannies in which numerous fish can hide.

Soft-corals and sponges, in a variety of colours and shapes, garland tangled steel and decaying hulls of even the most utilitarian of vessels unfortunate enough to have ended up on the sea-bed. Red, orange, pink, blue, white are all represented whilst growth-forms range from thin encrustations to massive and intricately formed vases or draping branches. Pearl oysters, scallops and clams are often found attached to such wrecks, frequently over-grown by sponges. Delicate, miniature fern-like hydroids may give surfaces a superficially 'furry' appearance and the unwary diver may discover to his cost that these are in fact small hydroids such as *Lytocarpus*, capable of inflicting quite painful stings. Another dominant feature of the underwater scene around the Emirates' shoreline is that of sea-weeds, especially brown *Sargassum* and the fan-leafed *Padina* weed.

Divers tend to be especially wary of sea-urchins such as the black-spined *Diadema setosum*, an algal grazing species which seeks shade in daytime, either hiding under ledges or sometimes simply joins with other Diademas to form massive, dense black aggregations. They have every cause to take care since *Diadema* spines are finely serrated and almost impossible to extract from the skin. The greatest danger from these, as indeed from several other potentially harmful creatures such as Stonefish, occurs when one is in shallow water, generally wading in or out of the sea. For this reason it is advisable to protect oneself by wearing shoes and possibly also an old pair of trousers. There are in fact several species of venomous fish in the Emirates. Lionfish (*Pterois*) are usually admired for their brightly coloured delicate fin extensions and unsuspecting swimmers have been known to actually try to touch these fish which are capable of inflicting a powerful sting. Stonefish, characterised by a large, ugly head, cavernous mouth and well camouflaged body bearing a row of poisonous spines, are very difficult to see underwater. The Black-spined Stonefish (*Pseudosynanceia melanostigma*) frequently lies in very shallow pools, in less than six inches of water, whilst the Reef Stonefish, (*Synanceia verrucosa*) is equally well camouflaged and very dangerous. These species have recently been reviewed in another book by Immel Publishing (Red Sea Safety; Vine, 1986).

A Moray Eel challenges the photographer with gaping jaws at five metres, off Fujairah's coastline. (Woodward)

The Gulf is quite renowned for its sea-snakes, nine species of which occur in UAE waters. The main forms are the yellow-bellied (*Pelamis platurus*), the Reef Sea-snake (*Hydrophis ornatus*), the Blue-banded Sea-snake (*H. cyanocinctus*), Arabian Gulf Sea-snake (*H. lapemoides*) and the Yellow Sea-snake (*H. spiralis*). Since sea-snakes are of course cold blooded air-breathing reptiles, they often float at the surface, warming themselves in the sunlight. The Yellow-bellied Sea-snake performs this function while apparently pretending to be a piece of floating wood: when small fish approach, they are rapidly devoured. Each species occupies a particular niche, and there appears also to be well established migratory routes and breeding seasons. Most sea-snakes shed their skin about once every three or four weeks, helping to rid themselves of any encrusting organisms like barnacles. They have a remarkable capacity for remaining underwater for long periods: dives of two hours have been recorded, a feat achieved by virtue of their ability to actually store air in an elongate right lung, incorporating an air sac which serves as both swim-bladder and reserve air-supply.

Also reptiles, but far less threatening in their demeanour, turtles may be encountered along both coastlines of the UAE. The Green Turtle (*Chelonia mydas*), weighing up to 160 or so kilograms eats sea-grasses whilst the smaller Hawksbill (*Eretmochelys imbricata*) is only herbivorous during its juvenile phase, with adults eating sponges, molluscs and other invertebrates. Loggerhead turtles (*Dermochelys coriacea*) and the Olive Ridley (*Lepidochelys olivacea*) also occur in the Gulf of Oman where important nesting sites exist at Ras Al Hadd and Masirah Island. Observations coordinated by the Emirates Natural History Group list records for Green Turtles at Khor Kalba, Jazirat Badiyah and Das Island; a Loggerhead at Da'biyah; and a large Leathery Turtle on the beach at Hamriya.

One may find many interesting places to dive in the UAE. Just off the east coast, between Khor Fakkan and Dibba, lies Sharma Rock, a small reef area offering a wide variety of Indian Ocean marine-life, differing from that inside the Gulf. The rock itself is quite small and can be circumnavigated by swimmers in less than an hour. At the very edge of the tideline, *Bulla mauritiana*, a member of the whelk family, with a large white extended foot and a cumbersome shell on its back, occurs. In shallow-water there are hosts of olive shells and basket-whelks whilst rays, Leopard Flounder, Spotted Sole and eels also abound. Among the latter category, the Yellow-finned Snake-eel, *Brachysomophis cirrhocheilus*, inhabits deep holes in the sand, from which it emerges from time to time. Under stones one may find nemertean worms, scale-worms, burrowing ceri-anthid anemones and many molluscs including cowries and potentially dangerous cone-shells such as *Conus striatus*. Unlike the well-mixed water body in the Gulf, divers on the east coast may experience sharp thermoclines, where a distinct fall in temperature occurs between a generally warmer upper layer and a cooler deep layer.

Along the west coast of the UAE, off Ras Al Khaimah, extensive sea-grass beds in shallow protected bays offer interesting marine-life such as sea-horses and soft bodied molluscan sea-hares, particularly numerous during their breeding season. Here too, the cowrie, *Cypraea lentignosa*, may be observed laying masses of tiny orange eggs. Wentletraps such as *Epitonium irregulare* can also be seen laying strings of dull coloured eggs, joined together by an elastic-like thread. Shoals of silver-barred Halfbeaks, *Hemiramphus marginatus* excavate the sandy bottom in search for food while the odd sinister visitor in the shape of a black-tipped reef-shark may glide past, having arrived from deeper offshore waters. Graceful cuttlefish swim by while the occasional turtle flaps into view and large, menacing Barracuda patrol their patch.

The Gulf is home for one species whose ecology remains quite a mystery to marine biologists in the area. The shy, reclusive sea-cow or Dugong referred to in Arabic as **Arus el Bahar** or 'sea-bride'

Close-up of *Dendronephthya* soft coral at Dibba Island, Fujairah. (Woodward)

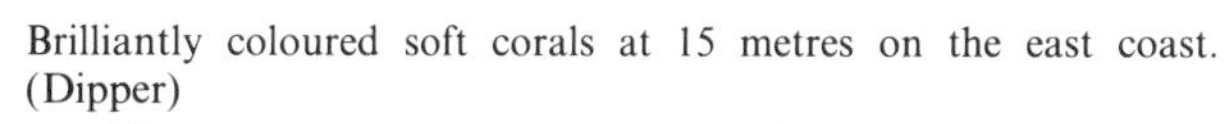

Brilliantly coloured soft corals at 15 metres on the east coast. (Dipper)

is apparently staging something of a come-back in the region. Despite the best efforts of Man to scare the legendary beasts away by underwater explosions; to drown them in fishing nets; to starve them by in-filling of coastal sea-grass beds; or to make them flee with oil-spills; the gentle Dugong lives-on, and gathers from time to time in remarkably big herds. Early in 1986, for example, over six hundred Dugong were counted in a herd feeding between Bahrain and Qatar. There is no doubt that these sea-mammals have been an important feature of local-life for many thousands of years. Excavations at the settlement of Umm an Nar revealed Dugong bones, proving that they were used for food as early as 2700 BC. Today, all the Gulf States agree that this reclusive sea-mammal should receive total protection, and it is to be sincerely hoped that they will indeed survive in the area despite the tremendous threats to their existence.

Dugongs are not however the only marine-mammals to inhabit UAE waters. Whales occasionally become stranded on local beaches. Recently, near Kalba on the east coast, fifteen fishermen using five boats towed in a ten ton weight, 12 metre long unidentified whale. Cetaceans sighted in UAE waters include Bryde's Whale, Fin, Humpback, False Killer, Killer and Pygmy Killer; whilst Blue Whale have been sighted off the Aden coast and may occasionally pass through the region. A likely place from which to watch dolphins is Dubai's Jebel Ali Hotel, where they can often be seen within several metres of the main jetty, especially during calm early morning periods. Recorded dolphins and porpoises include the Finless Porpoise (*Neophocaena phocaenoides*), Risso's Dolphin (*Grampus griseus*), Spotted, Striped and Spinner Dolphins (i.e. *Stenella attenuata*, *S. coeruleoalba*, and *S. longirostris*); Common Dolphins (*Delphinus delphis*), Indo-Pacific Humpback Dolphins (*Sousa chinensis*) and the Bottle-nosed Dolphin (*Tursiops truncatus*).

Nudibranch on colonial sea-squirts off Jumeira, Dubai, at approximately 5 metres. (Woodward)

Work by local naturalists, members of the Emirates Natural History Group, based in Abu Dhabi, has helped to keep track of local dolphins. Their 'Dolphin Watch' team record sightings and any other relevant information and this is sent to the Dolphin Survey Project based at Cambridge University. Sightings almost always coincide with the presence of fish schools. Over a six month period, 271 dolphins were sighted in the area of the Zakum oil field, while 510 were recorded in the Umm Saif field. There have been many instances of dolphins grounding themselves in shallow water along the UAE coastline, frequently resisting well-meaning attempts to return them to deep-water. Often, such creatures appear to be uninjured and it is indeed heart-rending to watch them dying. On other occasions, however they may show signs of struggles, and dead dolphins are often half-eaten by sharks. Whether the sea-mammal died before the shark attacked however is generally not clear. Certainly, healthy dolphins are well able to fend off sharks.

BIRDS

The sub-continent of Arabia is a migratory cross-roads for numerous birds as they fly between Asia, Africa and Europe. At certain times of year vast numbers may be observed, resting in oases, or beating their way along invisibly defined migratory routes. The Emirates, with its indented coastline, ever expanding areas of greenery in the form of gardens and agricultural projects, together with wild and relatively undisturbed desert and mountain locations, offers a wide variety of habitats for numerous birds. Between August and October the main passage routes are from Eurasia to Africa and from Europe to India or Africa. In many cases their routes pass over the UAE or else birds from colder northern climes actually over-winter in the Emirates. Their return northwards occurs from February to April.

Much of the data on local birds has been amassed by enthusiastic amateur bird-watchers whose efforts have been coordinated by Natural History Societies in the UAE. Their work has led

Backbone of a whale washed-up on the beach provides a reminder of the marine mammals which inhabit UAE waters but whose presence is rarely observed by the local populace. (Furley)

to the recording of three hundred and thirty five species, comprising resident breeding birds, passage migrants, winter visitors, summer breeding visitors and vagrants. At a time when suitable habitats for wildlife are being increasingly encroached on by Man's activities, it is worth noting that here, in the UAE, there has been a recent increase in the amount of bird-life. This is a direct result of the extensive irrigation and planting which is gradually transforming huge areas of the UAE into green cultivated land where birds can find both water and food. Despite its warm climate and southerly location, an increasing number of what we regard as common European garden birds are appearing in the UAE. Mild winters are not so far removed from the warm weather of an English summer, and Robins, Bramblings, Starlings, or Song Thrushes are increasing in numbers as local gardens are developed.

Birds of Gardens and Parks

The numerous parks and gardens of the UAE provide shade and food for avian visitors and locally breeding species. Recent expansion of horticulture has even encouraged many previous visiting species to remain in the UAE and to forego their northerly migrations. The Kestrel, Indian Roller and Indian Silverbill fall into this category. Song Thrushes are primarily winter visitors, arriving in November, towards the end of the peak southerly migration period, and remaining until late March when, once again they fly north to temperate climes.

Pale Crag Martins, normally occurring in steep-sided wadis and among rugged mountains, may now be seen catching insects around local gardens, particularly at the impressive gardens of Hatta Fort Hotel. This magnificent location also provides a habitat for Purple Sunbirds which may be seen as they gather nectar from Vitex bushes. Bulbuls and Graceful Warblers also frequent such gardens, as do numerous Brown-Necked Ravens and House Sparrows. The latter have spread rapidly throughout the Emirates during the past decade.

Local city gardens often harbour Grey Francolin, Skylarks, pipits, swallows and a number of other birds, augmented by the escape of exotic captive species, such as the Common Mynah, Ring-necked Parakeet and the Red-vented Bulbul. Fears that such introduced species may eventually oust local species are well founded, particularly with respect to the Common Mynah which is aggressive towards other birds and a frequent culprit of attacks on indigenous birds' nests.

On occasions, gardens or parks in the UAE may receive visits from relatively rare species. A Black Francolin, a non- migratory species whose nearest breeding grounds are in southern Iraq and south-west Iran, was recently sighted in Abu Dhabi. In September 1984, there was considerable local interest in the arrival of 200–300 White Storks which took up residence at Abu Dhabi International Airport where most of them stayed until January 1985. Also in 1985, three Mute Swans visited the sewage farm near Abu Dhabi. Other unusual sightings include Icterine Warblers, a Rustic Bunting and Savi's Warblers.

BIRDS

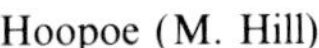

Hoopoe (M. Hill).

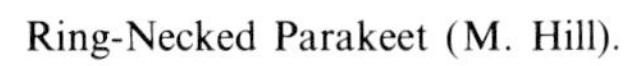

Ring-Necked Parakeet (M. Hill).

Greater Flamingos (M. Hill).

Hoopoe Lark (M. Hill).

Blue-cheeked Bee-eater (M. Hill).

European Bee-eater (M. Hill).

Graceful Warbler at nest (M. Hill).

Lesser Crested Terns (M. Hill).

Socotra Cormorant colony (M. Hill).

Red-Billed Tropicbird (M. Hill).

Saffa Park lies just outside the city of Dubai, hidden among desert wasteland and scrub, and providing an attractive oasis for many birds. Two hundred and thirty different species have been recorded here (from a total UAE bird-list of 335). The one kilometre square park, open to the public, is tended by a team of gardeners aided by an efficient sprinkler irrigation system. Native trees such as Acacia, gum and tamarisk provide valuable shade and resting places for numerous migrating birds; whilst an artificial lake offers a plentiful supply of fresh-water. During wintertime one can probably count, without much effort, twenty or thirty species of birds around this lake. During April, large numbers of Hoopoes, Great Grey Shrikes or European Bee-eaters are common; the latter attracted by swarming bees.

Birds of Dubai Creek

Waders and passage migrants are attracted to the shallow water and nutritious mud-flats of Dubai Creek: regarded as one of the most important avian sites in southern Arabia. The creek extends inland for about ten kilometres, forming a large, eight hundred acre, shallow lagoon with an average depth of three to four metres. Protection of the lagoon shores (closed to the general public) has encouraged many birds to occupy the region on a more permanent basis whilst it continues to provide an important resting and feeding location for numerous passage migrants and winter visitors. Dredging within the lagoon has resulted in an improvement of water exchange and a consequent enhancement of it as a marine habitat. This in turn has led to the production of more food available to waders which come here in their thousands.

Along the edges of sand-banks, Dunlin and other small waders can be seen, probing the soft sediment for food. Lesser Golden Plovers, Grey Plovers, Curlew Sandpipers, Greenshank, Godwits and Redshank begin arriving in July and generally remain in the vicinity until April. Ducks are later arrivals, appearing in October. Ornithologists are especially protective towards, and interested in, the Ospreys which nest on uninhabited Gulf islands but regularly visit the creek to catch their prey; a most dramatic sight as they lunge with talons extended at the sea-surface, rising again on heavy wing-beats, miraculously gripping a struggling fish. Reef Herons are also resident at the creek, nesting among mangroves and stalking the shallows for fish to spear with their long beaks.

Towards the inner reaches of the creek it may be possible to see that most exquisitely formed wader, the Avocet, which is a passage migrant. They are frequently accompanied by an array of duck species including Teal, Garganey, Widgeon , Tufted Duck and Mallard.

Beyond any doubt however the real celebrities of Dubai Creek's burgeoning avian population are the Greater Flamingos. They are also the main reason for much of the environmental protection taking place around Dubai Creek, a process which has enhanced the area for a wide variety of species, including the magnificent Flamingos. Greater Flamingos are not known to have nested on the Arabian peninsula since 1922 and had never been known to breed in the Emirates. In 1985 there were more than 1,700 Greater Flamingos on the Creek, having arrived from their breeding sites in Turkey, Russia, Iran , Afghanistan and Pakistan. Although many of them indulged in elaborate mating displays and apparent nesting behaviour, none of them actually bred. Following this a decision was made to provide them with an especially constructed biologically suitable nesting site. Advice was sought from the British Trust for Ornithology who sent Dr Mike Moser as a consultant to the Dubai Government. Following his visit a breeding island was constructed, four hundred metres from the shore, away from any disturbance. At the time of writing this bold ecological experiment is proceeding with a high chance of success.

A recent survey of the bird-life of Dubai Creek has been carried out by a team from Durham University, on behalf of the Dubai Government. The five-week survey involved trapping, ringing, measuring and recording as many birds as possible (final count was 530 ringed birds belonging to 17 species). Birds were caught using night-set mist-nets which were strung up along flight-paths in the Creek. Among the species ringed, Dunlin, Curlew Sandpipers, Little Stints, Kentish Plovers, Red Shank, Greenshank and Bar-tailed Godwits predominated. Among the rarer birds caught was one Wood Sandpiper. The survey turned up one interesting and unexpected result in that 4,000 of the World's estimated 30,000 Broadbilled Sandpipers were discovered to inhabit the Creek; a fact which may lead to it being declared as an I.U.C.N. World Heritage Site.

Birds of Abu Dhabi's Eastern Lagoon Reserve

The Old Sewage Farm, situated in Abu Dhabi's Eastern Lagoon, is another important ornithological site in the Emirates. A recent declaration by H.H. Shaikh Zayed has declared that a new bird reserve will be formed, covering the mangroves and tidal-flats between Qasr Al Bahr and Batin Airport. No hunting, shooting or fishing is allowed in this area which is to be managed as a bird reserve. The credit for its establishment rests partially with the Emirates Natural History Group, based in Abu Dhabi, which conducted a survey of bird-life in the area and strongly argued the case for its protection.

Mangroves fringing the lagoon provide nesting sites for several species and important resting sites for passage migrants. On a single visit here one may see Teal, Reef Herons, Curlew, Whimbrel, Clamorous Reed Warblers, White Wagtails, Yellow Wagtails and Citrine Wagtails. The lagoon is also an important wintering site for Little Egrets, Marsh Harriers, Little Stints, Dunlin, Curlews and other waders. Some of the reserve's species, such as the Reef Heron, Little Green Heron and Clamorous Reed Warbler are now identified as resident breeders. Reef Herons build quite scrappy nests from twigs which are frequently placed in such a loosely formed matrix that their oval pale bluish-green eggs may be clearly seen from beneath the nest!

Clamorous Reed Warblers in the reserve build intricately woven cup-shaped nests from feathers, grass, fibrous material and bits of flotsam. They are generally lodged between three upright branchlets of a mangrove, and two to three eggs are laid.

Protection of Abu Dhabi's Eastern Lagoon is another positive step forward for wildlife conservation in the Emirates where an increasing appreciation of the importance of such projects provides hope for the future.

Birds of Deserts, Wadis and Mountains

A wide variety of habitats occur among the wild open spaces of the Emirates, ranging from desert steppe and scrub to isolated cliff-edges, caves and numerous hollows. Cretaceous shales of the gravel plains aligned along the edge of mountains offer ideally secluded habitats for such birds of prey as the Griffon, Egyptian and Lappet-faced Vultures which soar effortlessly on thermals created by heat rising from the desert plains. Except for the Egyptian Vulture, which is quite common around Al Ain and Hafit, these are relatively rare birds. High, rugged mountains bordering with Oman, are nesting sites for the Lappet-faced Vulture, Egyptian Vulture, Bonelli's Eagle and the Long-legged Buzzard.

Sand Partridge occur on the plains and have been recorded at up to 800 metres, among the hills. Little Owls are generally heard rather than seen; their haunting cries carrying far over the still cool evening air. Also among the scrub and rocks of the plains, are Rock Dove, Desert Larks, Hume's Wheatear and Scrub Warbler.

Villages situated along wadis, and among the mountains, may provide quite lush vegetation and abundant water, attracting such species as the resident Graceful Warbler, the Black-headed Bulbul, House Bunting and Palm Dove, a species which is its own worst enemy because of a habit of building nests which are extremely easy to find! Bright blue-feathered Indian Rollers are a not infrequent, and extremely pleasing sight both here, and among the palm groves of Ras Al Khaimah.

Among the true desert birds, mention must be made of the Black-crowned Finch Lark and Hoopoe Lark which frequently occur at great distances from a water source. Lichenstein's Sand Grouse, the Cream Coloured Courser and Stone Curlew and Houbara Bustard (now sadly almost locally extinct) are also desert species, whilst owls are also occasionally sighted, including the occasional Eagle Owl.

Coastal Birds

Coastlines of the Emirates provide a rich variety of habitats for birds, including off-lying islands, beaches, rocky cliffs, mangroves and various harbours. About two hundred of the Emirates' avian fauna are linked to the coastline , of which a few breed locally. The majority of non-resident coastal birds arrive from July onwards although at least one, the Yellow-Throated Sparrow, comes for the summer, turning up in March.

The coast from Qatar to Abu Dhabi has wide inter-tidal sand-flats suitable for many waders; whilst the lagoon complex of Umm Al Quwain was an important breeding area for herons, terns and gulls, prior to its recent designation for development. Northern Ras Al Khaimah is fringed by a long sandy shore-line with intermittent mangrove outcrops, and backed by craggy mountains whose sedimentary origins are portrayed in twisted and buckled rock strata. Rams, not far from the Emirate's northern border with Oman, has several mangrove stands which have been proposed as reserves for breeding of herons and perhaps Flamingos.

The creek at Kalba, ten miles south of Fujairah, on the east coast, also has dense mangroves inhabited by a variety of herons and waders. This unique habitat, presently threatened with development, is the home of the White-collared Kingfisher, only twenty-three individuals of which have been counted, rendering it one of the world's rarest sub-species. This bird's dark green back, white collar and pale chest are distinctive features, as it perches on dead mangrove stumps or branches, intently scanning the water for fish to deftly spear with its long black bill. The European Kingfisher is another winter visitor to Khor Kalba where it hunts for fish while its brilliant turquoise and blue plumage flashes in the sunlight.

The Little Green Kingfisher, not quite as flamboyant in colouring as the European Kingfisher, with dullish green plumage, greyish on upper parts and a dark green crown, also occurs at Kalba. Rather a furtive bird, it creeps around after its prey in a rather diffident manner, before jabbing at the fish or crabs. It mainly feeds at dusk, perched on the lower branches of a mangrove tree, poised just above the water surface from where it is able to stab at passing fish.

Other birds visiting the UAE coast include the Red-necked Phalarope, a coastal passage migrant and small aquatic wader which takes to the land only during its breeding season, wintering in the Arabian Sea, often in large flocks. Other birds in this category include the White Pelican, Shearwaters, Sandwich Terns, Caspian Terns, White-cheeked Terns, Gull-billed Terns, Bridled Terns, Lesser Crested Terns, Common Terns, Lesser Black-backed Gulls, Herring Gulls, Slender-billed Gulls, Sooty Gulls, Black-headed Gulls, and Masked Boobies.

Birds of Offshore Islands

Socotra Cormorants, sometimes in huge flocks numbering up to 30,000 occur on islands belonging to the Emirates such as Arzahah (c.500); Qarneyn and Zirkuh (20,000 to 30,000). They are infested by ticks which cause fever in humans.

The island of Qarneyn also supports more than 200 pairs of Red-billed Tropicbirds, nesting in holes or crevices at ground-level, and laying a single egg which hatches around November to December. Sooty Gulls occurring here have the habit of feeding their young on the eggs and chicks of neighbouring tern colonies, the first gulls hatching just as the terns begin laying. Four species of tern nest on the island; i.e. the Swift, Lesser Crested, Bridled and White-cheeked. Other birds sighted here include Grey Herons; Kestrels; Nightjars; Common Cranes; Stints; Dunlin and plovers, together with a resident breeding pair of Ospreys whose three foot high nest contains rags, seaweed, rope, an old broomhead and part of an accumulator plate!

The privately owned Siniyah island, off Umm Al Quwain, is an important breeding site for up to 20,000 Socotra Cormorants whilst passage migrant Crab Plovers are also to be found feeding among mangroves in the lagoon.

Das Island, a small rocky island, approximately two miles square, is situated 165 kilometres north-west of Abu Dhabi and 135 kilometres east of Doha. Although industrialised and heavily populated, the island attracts wayward migrants and disorientated vagrants, together with a resident coastal breeding bird population. Cultivated gardens on the island attract swallows, Red-throated Pipits, Water Pipits, White Wagtails, olivaceous Warblers, Turtle Doves, Black-Headed Buntings and the Yellow-throated Sparrow.

BREEDING BIRDS OF THE UNITED ARAB EMIRATES*

(*compiled from information supplied by Colin Richardson and Effie Warr)

COMMON NAME	LATIN NAME	STATUS
Red-billed Tropicbird	*Phaethon aethereus*	RB.[Islands off w.coast.Eggs Dec-June]
Socotra Cormorant	*Phalacrocorax nigrogularis*	RB.[Islands off w.coast.Eggs Oct-Mar.]
Little Green Heron	*Butorides striatus*	RB.[Coastal. Eggs June and July]
Reef Heron	*Egretta gularis*	RB.[Coastal. Eggs April & June]
Egyptian Vulture	*Neophron percnopterus*	RB.[Mountain areas. Eggs March]
Lappet-faced Vulture	*Torgos tracheliotus*	RB.[Mountain areas.Eggs in Jan.]
Long-legged Buzzard	*Buteo rufinus*	RB.[Mountain areas.Eggs March]
Osprey	*Pandion haliaetus*	RB/WV [Coastal. Breeds on islands. Eggs Nov-Dec]
Kestrel	*Falco tinnunculus*	RB/WV.[Nests located.? Egg months]
Sooty Falcon	*Falco concolor*	MB.[Coastal on islands off w.coast]
Bonelli's Eagle	*Hieraaetus fasciatus*	RB.[Mountain areas]

Sand Partridge	*Ammoperdix heyi*	RB.[Mountains and foothills]
Grey Francolin	*Francolinus pondicerianus*	RB.[Foothills]
Houbara	*Chlamydotis undulata*	RB/WV.[Late Sept–Mid March. Scarce. Small breeding population under protection.]
Cream-coloured Courser	*Cursorius cursor*	RB.[Open sandy and gravel areas]
Little Ringed Plover	*Charadrius dubius*	MB.[Only absent in Dec.]
Kentish Plover	*C.alexandrinus*	RB/WV.[Likes water, normally coastal
Red-wattled Lapwing	*Hoploperus indicus*	RB.[Mountain wadis & foothills]
Sooty (Hemprich's)	*Gull Larus hemprichii*	RBorMB [Mostly late April-Sept]
Swift Tern	*Sterna bergii* MB.[Scarce from Nov-Feb]	
Lesser Crested Tern	*Sterna bengalensis*	MB.[Mostly May-Sept]
White-cheeked Tern	*Sterna* repressa	MB. [Mostly April-early Nov.]
Bridled Tern	*Sterna anaethetus*	MB. [Mostly late March-Sept; especially E.coast]
Saunders' Little Tern	*Sterna saundersi*	MB. [April–October]
Lichtenstein's Sandgrouse	*Pterocles lichtensteinii*	RB. [Mountain areas and gravel plains]
Chestnut-bellied Sandgrouse	*Pterocles exustus*	
Rock Dove	*Columba livia*	RB. [Mountains]
Collared Dove	*Streptopelia decaocto*	RB. [Common]
Palm Dove	*S.senegalensis*	RB. [Common]
Rose-ringed Parakeet	*Psittacula krameri*	RB. [Plantations]
Eagle Owl	*Bubo bubo*	RB. [Widespread]
Barn Owl	*Tyto alba*	RB. [Scarce]
Little Owl	*Athene noctua*	RB. [Near Mts]
Pallid Swift	*Apus pallidus*	RB. [Common]
White-collared Kingfisher	*Halcyon chloris*	RB. [East coast mangroves]
Little Green Bee-eater	*Merops orientalis*	RB. [Not west of Dubai]
Indian Roller	*Coracias benghalensis*	RB [prefers mountain areas]
Black-crowned Finch Lark	*Eremopterix nigriceps*	RB. [Desert & coastal strip]
Desert Lark	*Ammomanes deserti*	RB. [Near mountain areas]
Hoopoe Lark	*Alaemon alaudipes*	RB. [Widespread]
Crested Lark	*Galerida cristata*	RB. [Widespread]
African Rock Martin (=Pale Crag Martin)	*Ptyonoprogne fuligula*	RB. [Mountains]
White-cheeked Bulbul	*Pycnonotus leucogenys*	RB. [Plantations]
Black-capped Bulbul	*P.xanthopygos*	RB. [Mountains & westwards to Abu Dhabi]
Red-Vented Bulbul	*P.cafer*	RB. [Plantations]
Hume's Wheatear	*Oenanthe alboniger*	RB. [Mountains & sometimes coastal plains]
Rufous Bush Chat	*Cercotrichas galactotes*	MB [Widespread]
Graceful Warbler	*Prinia gracilis*	RB [Coastal and plantations]
Scrub Warbler	*Scotocerca inquieta*	RB [Mountains]
Olivaceous Warbler	*Hippolais pallida*	MB [Coastal]
Arabian Babbler	*Turtoides squamiceps*	RB [Widespread]
Purple Sunbird	*Nectarinia asiatica*	RB [Widespread]
Great Grey Shrike	*Lanius excubitor*	RB/WV [Widespread]
Indian House Crow	*Corvus splendens*	RB [Coastal and plantations]
Brown-necked Raven	*Corvus ruficollis*	RB [Widespread]
Common Mynah	*Agridotheres tristris*	RB [Plantations]
Bank Mynah	*A.ginginianus*	RB [Plantations]
House Sparrow	*Passer domesticus*	RB [Widespread]
Yellow-throated sparrow	*Petronia xanthocollis*	MB [Not recorded west of Dubai, but inc. Das Is.]
Indian Silverbill	*Euodice malabarica*	RB [Mountains]
House Bunting	*Emberiza striolata*	RB [Mountains & gravel plains]

RB = Resident Breeder
WV = Winter Visitor
MB = Migrant Breeder

Lizards. (Furley)

REPTILES

The Reptilian fauna of the United Arab Emirates is similar to that of Southern Arabia in general, comprising a variety of snakes together with skinks, geckos and other lizards, including the large Spiny-tailed Lizard or Dhabb, and the even larger Monitor Lizard together with marine turtles. Whilst many types of wildlife find survival in these hot arid conditions difficult or impossible, reptiles may actually flourish in desert environments where almost the only commodities which are not in short supply are the sun's burning heat and sand. Since reptiles (unlike mammals) do not use food-derived energy for maintenance of their body temperature, but instead bask in the sun to warm-up or hide in the shade to cool down, they require relatively little food and are able to survive for long periods without eating.

Lizards are seen wherever one goes, around the house, in the garden, in cultivated areas, across the desert or in the hills and mountains. The largest of these is the Grey Monitor reaching up to five feet in length and is a voracious predator of smaller lizards and rodents. A more frequently sighted large lizard is the Dhabb of which two or three species are present. These agile Agamids have a prehistoric appearance and an impressive ability to alter their colour; something they may do when alarmed, or more naturally over the course of the day when their light-sensitive skin can change from a dark grey to brilliant yellow. Sand skinks such as the Arabian Sand Skink are also found here, displaying numerous adaptations to their desert environment, including fringed scales on toes which prevent them from sinking into soft sand when they run. The Ocellated Skink and several *Mabuya* skinks prefer moister conditions, frequenting garden compost mounds. Among the true desert lizards, Lacertids are well represented with three main forms present; i.e. the Spiny -foot Lacertids, which live in sandy areas; the Desert Lacertids occupying firmer ground while the Lacertas are restricted to moist places near the summits of the mountains in neighbouring Oman. Apart from the Dhabb, there are several other Agama lizards including the Arabian Toad-head (on soft sand) and the Banded Toad-head (on gravel plains and sabkhas).

In contrast to most of the above species which are active during daytime, geckos, as their large eyes and soft skin suggest, are nocturnal creatures. House geckos, belonging to the genus *Hemidactylus* are extremely appealing and fascinating lizards, welcome in many homes throughout the UAE.

Snakes are not seen often in the wild in the UAE, partly because of the relatively sparse population and partly due to their cryptic behaviour. Most of the venomous species are vipers, with Burton's Carpet Viper (*Echis coloratus*), the Sand viper (*Cerastes cerastes*), and the Saw-scaled Viper (*Echis carinatus*) all represented. Burton's Carpet Viper is reported to inhabit moist wadis and irrigated plantations where it feeds on toads (*Bufo orientalis*), particularly among the Oman foothills.

The Sand Viper on the other hand lives in dry sandy areas,feeding on rodents and lizards. Jayakara's Sand Boa also lives in loose dry sand, and is a nocturnal species depending upon its ability to squeeze its prey rather than poison it. Mention should also be made of that strange creature, part snake, part lizard, an Amphisbaenian: a limbless, cylindrically bodied reptile whose body is marked by concentric grooves. It spends most of its time underground, feeding on insects. The false Cobra or Moila Snake, *Malpolon moilensis* lives in rocky country and has a habit of extending its neck when alarmed. The Sand Snake, *Psammophis schokari*, has a thin, striped body, pale ventrally and brown and yellow along its flanks. It feeds on birds and lizards, frequently climbing trees in pursuit of its prey.

Sea-snakes are also common in the seas bordering the UAE, where the Blue-banded *Hydrophis cyanocinctus* and Arabian Gulf Sea-snake *H. lapemoides*, prowl the sea-bed in search of food, usually in the shape of an unwary fish. Two other members of the same genus are also present; the Reef Sea-snake, *H. ornatus* and the Yellow Sea-snake, *H. spiralis* whilst the pelagic Yellow-bellied Sea-snake *Pelamis platurus*, is also recorded but seems to be much less common than *Hydrophis* species. Despite their awesome reputation, sea-snakes are not generally aggressive.

The other marine reptiles present in coastal waters are turtles, including the Green Turtle (*Chelonia mydas*), the Hawksbill (*Eretmochelys imbricata*), the Loggerhead (*Dermochelys coriacea*) and the Olive Ridley (*Lepidochelys olivacea*). Important nesting sites for the latter occur at Ras al Hadd and Masirah island.

Amphibians are relatively rare in the UAE but this toad, *Bufo orientalis* inhabits wadis and irrigated areas where its faint grunting call may be heard in daytime. (Furley)

MAMMALS

The Arabian desert, despite its apparently inhospitable conditions for wildlife, is inhabited by a remarkable variety of mammals. In his excellent study on this subject, David Harrison lists fifty species known to occur in the Gulf region and most of these have been recorded within the Emirates. These desert mammals are of particular interest to biologists since they show fascinating adaptations enabling them to survive on very little water and to contend with temperature extremes.

Among the order Insectivora, two families are present in the Emirates, shrews and hedgehogs. The Indian House Shrew occurs in association with Man, frequently in port areas, and has been introduced by sea, originally from India. Despite its superficial rat-like appearance it can be recognised as a shrew by its long pointed snout and minute eyes. It is a nocturnal mammal which may sometimes be seen around rubbish tips. Hedgehogs are perhaps more endearing to the general public, and two species occur locally, i.e. the Ethiopian Hedgehog which has a characteristic dark snout and smart white band on its forehead; and the much less common Brandt's Hedgehog. Both species appear to be virtually water-independent, living in extremely arid areas of the desert or escarpments. More recently, they have appeared in increasing numbers in local gardens and parks, often hiding under rocks or in hollows. Their heat control mechanisms are quite unusual in that the Ethiopian Hedgehog's long legs are regarded as important contributors towards cooling, permitting cold night air to ventilate the underside of its body as it pursues its nocturnal activities. Large ears are used in several mammals as a cooling device and this is true of Brandt's Hedgehog. Hedgehogs are unfortunately often collected from the wild and kept as pets, usually in the mistaken belief that they will be "better off". Such pets not infrequently give birth to young and these have soft spines, feeding from their mothers for a few weeks before the spines harden and they are able to fend for themselves.

There are several species of bats in the Emirates and both sub-orders of *Chiroptera* occur here: *Megachiroptera* or Fruit bats and *Microchiroptera*, of which five familes are found in the region; Mouse-Tailed Bats, Leaf-Nosed Bats, Vespertilionid Bats, Horseshoe Bats and Sheath-tailed Bats. The largest species is undoubtedly the Egyptian Fruit Bat (*Rousettus aegyptiacus*) which roosts in caves and darkened recesses of old ruined buildings. It occurs among the fruit growing areas of Ras Al Khaimah peninsula where it is regarded as a pest. Mouse-tailed Bats (*Rhinopoma muscatellum*), recognisable from their undulating bird-like flight, are often found living in caves, especially near Ras al Khaimah and Buraimi. The Trident Leaf-nosed Bat (*Asellia tridens*) is probably one of the most widespread bats in the Emirates and has relatively long ears, together with a characteristic nose-flap over the muzzle. It is a colonial species occurring in underground tunnels or caverns, especially irrigation channels forming part of the falaj system. Harrison aptly describes their flight as "butterfly-like". A related species, the Persian Leaf-Nosed Bat (*Triaenops persicus*) is less widespread but known to occur in water falaj tunnels at Al Ain and in the Buraimi oasis. Kuhl's Pipistrelle (*Pipistrellus kuhli*) is the smallest of the locally occurring bats, and is especially common around house gardens and in parks. It roosts in cracks and crevices of buildings and is a frequent sight in the evening around houses in the Emirates. Finally, mention should be made of the reclusive, and much less common, large species, Hemprich's Long-eared Bat (*Otonycteris hemprichi*) which occurs in desert areas and is recognisable from its large ears and pale greyish-white fur. Harrison makes the additional observation that males possess a peculiarly shaped phallus, resembling: "*a boot projecting from a boxing glove*"! Remains of this species have been discovered in pellets of birds of prey in a cave near Ras Al Khaimah.

Among the order Carnivora, thirteen species occur in the Gulf region as a whole, with the majority having been recorded, albeit in small numbers, from the UAE. The Desert Wolf (*Canis lupus*) has been seen in the vicinity of Buraimi and Jebel Hafit and it is believed that it is interbreeding with local dogs. In 1984 one entered Al Ain Zoo with a pack of dogs and was unfortunately shot. By far the most widespread carnivore in the region is the Common Red Fox (*Vulpes vulpes*). Hiding in holes and burrows during daytime, it emerges at night to feed on a very wide variety of food items ranging from small birds, lizards or mammals to fruit and even insects. Ruppell's Sand Fox (*Vulpes ruppelli*) is somewhat smaller than the Red Fox and has prominent ears, the outer tips of which lack the black markings characterising the Red Fox. This species is essentially a desert creature, rarely seen close to human habitation. Among its adaptations, enabling it to cope with the extreme heat of its chosen environment, are a pair of large ears whose inner surface are lined by minute capillaries enabling cooling of the blood. A skull of this species was discovered in the Jebel Ali region of Dubai in 1973 but there are very few sightings reported. The smallest of the desert foxes is the dainty Fennec Fox (*Fennecus zerda*) which has pale coloured fur, large ears and a bushy tail with a prominent black tip. Despite several reports of this species from the UAE, it seems likely that these are in fact mistaken identifications of Ruppell's Sand Fox.

The elusive and mysterious Striped Hyaena is known to occur in the Emirates but sightings have been very sparse. A striped coat and dog-like build

A captive Sand Cat, *Felis margarita* displays the characteristic features of this now rare species, such as broad feet, enabling it to move rapidly over soft sand, and low ears, which it flattens when stalking its prey. (H. Eller)

The Arabian Tahr is a species of wild goat whose status in the UAE is uncertain. (Usher-Smith)

render it unmistakable but it is extremely shy, nocturnal, hiding in underground dens during day time, and is rarely seen by Man. The most recent sighting of it in the UAE was in 1985 around Hatta. Wild Cats, belonging to a distinct species, *Felis sylvestris*, occur locally with the subspecies: *Felis sylvestris tristrami* reported from Dubai and Gordon's Wild Cat (*Felis sylvestris gordoni*) occurring in local deserts; while the related Sand Cat (*Felis margarita harrisoni*) is known from the Abu Dhabi—Qatar border area. All are nocturnal hunters feeding primarily on small birds, rodents and reptiles.

Unfortunately all wild-cats in the UAE have suffered from hunting and may now be approaching local extinction. In addition to the species mentioned above, this applies also to the Caracal Lynx (*Caracal caracal schmitzi*), a medium sized cat recognisable from its reddish/sandy colour and the absence of any body pattern. It lives around the base of mountains and on dry steppe lands where it is well camouflaged, a fact which, together with its reclusive behaviour, renders it very difficult to see in the wild. It is a powerful and impressive hunter, able to bring down a bird in flight, and unfortunately implicated in attacks on domestic livestock, inevitably leading to it being hunted and virtually wiped out from the region. Recent reports refer to a sighting at Tawi Suwaihan, north-west of Buraimi; one found near Dubai; a female shot in 1985, ten kilometres north of Dibba, and a male shot at Rams in 1986.

Whether there are still any Arabian Leopards (*Panthera pardus nimr*) among the mountains of Ras Al Khaimah peninsula is a moot point. There are some individuals living in the Musandam region of Oman where they are carefully protected and it does seem likely that individuals occasionally cross over into the UAE. Sightings by local villagers are however difficult to interpret since they refer to such cats as **Nimr,** a term they apply equally to Lynx. If the Leopard is still living in the Emirates, the place to search for it is undoubtedly among the hills and mountains of the Ras Al Khaimah-Oman border country, far from any human settlements.

Wild ungulates of the Emirates include the Arabian Tahr, Arabian Oryx, Goitered Gazelle, Dorcas Gazelle, the Mountain Gazelle, and a single sighting of a wild goat. A small group of Arabian Tahr (*Hemitragus jayakari*) was discovered by Wilfred Thesiger on Jebel Hafit, near Al Ain, in the early 1950's. A dead Tahr was found in the region in 1983 and a live one sighted in 1984, and again, more recently, in 1986. The latter sighting was on the summit of Jebel Hafit, now served by a new road, a fact which may well spell the end for this isolated population of shaggy haired, dark, beardless short horn goats. A reserve for them is operating in nearby Oman however and there are hopes for a local revival of the species.

The Arabian Oryx (*Oryx leucoryx*), was once abundant in the wild in the UAE and Philby reported seeing it in the western Manasir country. Captive herds in the Gulf region are producing sufficient animals to permit cautious reintroduction of them into the wild. This has already taken place in Oman where results are extremely promising. The Rheem or Goitered gazelle, (*Gazella subgutturosa marica*), is the typical sand desert gazelle of Arabia, where it is found feeding on desert succulents, its pale colour blending perfectly with the surroundings. The present century has brought the local population down to almost extinction with very few positive sightings in recent years. They were reported a few years ago at Hatta and it is believed that the only place, today, where these animals may be seen in the wild in the Emirates is along the Qatar/ Abu Dhabi border region and along the Saudi Arabian/UAE border, near the edge of the Empty Quarter. This species, along with the Arabian Mountain Gazelle or Idmi (*Gazella gazella*) survive in a semi-natural state on the privately owned and protected island of Al Siniyah off Umm Al Quwain. The latter species is by no means as rare as Rheem, and may be observed along the Abu Dhabi—Dubai road, not far from Jebel Ali; and in semi-desert scrub *Acacia* country of Abu Dhabi, particularly inland, from Hatta to Masafi. Despite local protection measures both these gazelle have suffered from hunting pressures. Before leaving the subject of gazelles in the UAE it is worth mentioning that Abu Dhabi means 'father of the gazelle' and the island was named as a result of a group of hunters who were tracking gazelle, eventually pursuing it onto the island now known as Abu Dhabi, where it led them to a previously unknown freshwater spring (believed to be at the site of the present Al Hisa Palace). It was this incident which led to the main settlement on the island.

The Cape Hare, *Lepus capensis*, is an adaptable small mammal occurring in many areas of the UAE, and showing a fair degree of local variation. It often hides in shallow scooped holes built in the sides of sand-hills, and is very difficult to see. The large-eared dull-grey coated sub-species, *L.c.omanensis*, lives in the mountains of the UAE, behind Sharjah.

An especially appealing small mammal, widely distributed in the UAE, is the Lesser Jerboa (*Jaculus jaculus*) which carries a distinctive black and white tipped tail. It is extremely well adapted for living in desert conditions, hibernating during intense heat, remaining in their burrows and surviving on stored food reserves. Captive jerboas do not require fresh water, but obtain their moisture from vegetable food. Another small rodent found in the UAE is the spiny mouse (*Acomys dimidiatus*), recorded from mountainous areas including Jebel Faiyah. Sundevall's Jird (*Meriones crassus*) is a small, nocturnal rodent, well adapted to desert life and not uncommon in the Emirates, mainly in sandy terrain and frequently in small colonies burrowing under thorn bushes. Its relative, the Libyan Jird (*Meriones libycus*) is, as its name suggests, a northern species, but it has been reported from Buraimi district. Both the Baluchistan Gerbil (*Gerbillus nanus*) and Wagner's Gerbil (*Gerbillus dasyurus*) live in the UAE. The former inhabits saline, flat sandy areas whilst the latter prefers rocky, mountainous terrain.

A Tower-Headed Grasshopper. (Furley)

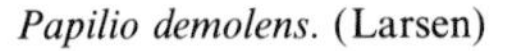

Papilio demolens. (Larsen)

INSECTS AND ARACHNIDS

The insect fauna of the UAE benefits from the wide range of habitats available, ranging from mountains to mangroves and deserts to city gardens. Not all the insects are permanent residents however, some are simply temporary visitors, driven by wind, or undertaking more purposeful migrations. Behavioural adaptations of many species include a tendency to seek shade during the middle of the day, emerging in the early morning and evening, or only at night.

Arachnids, comprising spiders, scorpions, false scorpions, harvestmen, mites and ticks are espe-

Danaus chrysippus. (Larsen)

Anapheis aurota. (Larsen)

cially well adapted to avoid dessication. Several forms have poisonous bites, and may prey upon insects, small mammals and even reptiles. Among the scorpions, the family *Buthidae* predominate with the dark brown or black scorpion considered to be the most poisonous, but neurotoxic bites are more commonly inflicted by the yellow species. Both forms hide under rocks, logs, or in crevices. The bedouin remedy for stings involves a poultice concocted from salt and garlic.

Despite its fierce appearance, the Camel Spider is not poisonous. When cornered it has an alarming turn of speed and is capable of delivering a painful, but not dangerous, bite. Members of the *Solifugae*, Camel Spiders owe their scientific designation to their dislike of direct sun-light (*Solifugae = sun-fleeing*). Camel Spiders are fascinating creatures with some remarkable capabilities. During their mating behaviour the smaller male induces its much larger mate into a state of catalepsy. This enviable ability is achieved by the male gently rubbing the female with its forelegs and pedipalps: once the female is apparently unconscious the male turns her over and rapidly deposits its sperm before the female starts to wake-up. Should the male linger too long, there is every chance that the female, upon regaining consciousness, will eat her erstwhile mate!

Of all the Emirates' flying insects, the most infamous is almost certainly the desert locust. The UAE lies between two large areas of locust activity; the Indo-Pakistan region and the countries bordering the Red Sea and Gulf of Aden. During major infestations, usually from September to November for locusts arriving from the east, or February to April for those coming from the west or southwest, locusts settle to breed in areas where at least 25mm of rain have fallen during the previous month. Locust control organisations have achieved considerable success in reducing the numbers of these pests capable of causing enormous crop damage. Their records indicate that major areas for locust hoppers in the UAE were Dubai, Sharjah, Ras Al Khaimah and Daid, although it must be stated that insect control work has largely eradicated risk from locust invasions. Pesticides are now used under careful control of the Ministry of Agriculture which has banned organochlorides such as DDT, Dieldrin and Clordane, widely used in the past.

Much of the entomological work in the UAE has been conducted by amateurs, especially members of the various Natural History groups. The Abu Dhabi based society has made a study of bees and wasps found in the UAE. Collections began in 1980 and in the first year they had found 185 species, several of which were new to science. The

Hypolimnas musippus. (Larsen)

small Asiatic Honeybee, *Apis florea*, was discovered in the new reserve area of Abu Dhabi's eastern lagoon. Among the wasps, members of the Sphecoidea, or digging wasps, are quite common in plantations and wadis where they may nest in tree hollows or among sand. Hornets such as the large brown and yellow *Vespa orientalis* and *Polistes walt* are relatively common near fresh-water, particularly around Hatta and Dibba.

Among the most attractive elements of the UAE's insect fauna are its moths and butterflies of which there are a wide variety represented. The Painted Lady Butterfly, familiar to Europeans, forms huge colourful swarms during its migratory phase. Other forms include the Lime Swallow-tail, the Desert White, Desert Orange-tip, Salmon Arab, Plain Tiger, Leopard and Caper White together with many others. Moths, primarily nocturnal, are less frequently seen by casual observers. Perhaps the most common species (and one which seems to have increased following extensive planting of oleanders) is the Oleander Hawkmoth (*Daphnis nerii*), a large green, pink and brown species with a three and a half inch wing-span.

Jundnia orithya. (Larsen)

Tarucus rosaceus. (Larsen)

TRADITIONS

People of the United Arab Emirates, in the face of extensive modernisation, place a high value on the traditional aspects of their cultural heritage. Their real strength of character, forged in a long-standing struggle to survive in the harsh desert environment, honed and reinforced by a deep religious faith, has stood the test of time and remains undiminished despite the surrounding trappings of wealth. In many ways, this is not quite as surprising as it may seem, since it is not so long ago that the region existed in a tribal state, dependent upon the camel for transport and word of mouth for communication of news: the deserts were the sole domain of bedouin tribes. It is the traditions of this period, as experienced both by nomadic and settled populations, that link the past to the present and provide a secure foundation for the future.

TRADITIONAL OCCUPATIONS

The rearing of livestock, including sheep and goats but especially camels, date-cultivation, seafaring, fishing and pearling were the economic

Camels waiting to be sold at bustling Al Ain Market. (Vine)

For many people in the UAE desert-life retains a strong attraction and the resourceful camel remains the most adaptable form of transport. (Vine)

mainstays of this region for many centuries. We have already alluded to the versatile tribesman who was himself a camel-breeder, date-grower, and pearl diver, or, at the very least, shared these skills with the members of his family. Nowhere was this life-saving adaptability more prevalent than in the egalitarian Bani Yas confederation of tribes inhabiting the lower Gulf. Having migrated into this area approximately three centuries ago, they gradually began to depend as much on the cultivation of dates in the Liwa oasis as they did on their original camel-breeding activities. Eventually attaining a semi-settled status, many took up pearling as an additional means of earning a living: like the rest of their ventures, this too was a communal effort. This doesn't mean that all the men of the Bani Yas took part in the whole range of these activities; one division of the tribe never went diving and others, like the Rumaithat, were mainly fishermen and have not taken part in date-cultivation in recent generations. Since these seasonal activities often coincided to some degree, for example, the date harvest overlapped with the summer pearling expedition, there had to be a great deal of co-ordination of activities in the family and within the tribal society as a whole. Members of a sub-tribe or associated group, for a set fee or payment in kind, herded camels or harvested dates as the occasion arose. The same degree of versatility and co-operative involvement in all the available economic resources was not as evident in the Buraimi oasis and the northern regions of the UAE. Unlike the majority of Bani Yas, the tribes of this region were rarely engaged in more than two occupations and individual or family ownership of resources using a "wage-earning class" as labour was much more common.

The enormous wealth generated from soaring oil revenues posed a deep threat to traditional occupations since the income emanating from these labour-intensive tasks could not hope to rival oil money. However the government of the UAE was ever aware of the inherent problems brought about by such prosperity and offered subsidies and incentives to promote and consolidate the traditional economy. Much has been preserved but is now structured in a slightly different way. Today the native population employs foreign labour as farmers, herdsmen, boat-builders and fishermen but still manages and controls these vital traditional occupations, the foundations on which the modern society has been built.

Camel-breeding

Domesticated about four thousand years ago in southern and central Arabia, the camel has always been the most important animal bred in this region. Very few tribes, living in or around the area covered by the UAE were exclusively camel-breeders, even the almost entirely bedouin Bani Qitab and the Manasir owned date gardens. But most of the Awamir and sections of the Rashid,

Manahil, Afar, Al Murrah and others centered their whole lives on their animals. Not only did the camel provide transport, milk, meat, wool, skin for water containers, belts, sandals and dung for fuel, but it was also a marketable resource used to acquire certain essentials such as rifles, clothes, rice, coffee, sugar or even jewellery. Winding camel caravans carrying goods for hundreds of miles were a familiar feature of this south-eastern corner of Arabia right through history. Today, the camel remains one of the pillar-stones of Arabian traditional life, gracing the wind-blown sands with her dignified presence. A legendary capacity for lengthy survival in the sandy wastes renders the animal ideally suited for the harsh, arid environment in which, together with the Bedouin, they exist.

Camels possess an interesting range of adaptations concerned with maintenance of water balance. In order to minimise loss through evaporation they turn their bodies, exposing the least body surface towards the sun, frequently grouping together. Even breathing is carefully controlled, avoiding intake of sand, and moistening inhaled air within the nasal cavity, while exhaled air is cooled prior to release, thus reducing water loss. Body temperature can rise to six degrees above normal before a camel begins to sweat. The hump is essentially a food store and, after a long arduous journey, a floppy hump may betray a camel's poor condition. Camels can travel for as long as 30 days without freshwater in the cool winter months; for ten to fifteen days without water in temperatures of 30 to 35 degrees centigrade; but at 40 degrees and over, periods between required water intake shorten. The precise length of time without water will of course depend on a number of factors including the kinds of plant grazed, the load carried, and the speed of the journey. On arrival at a water source, after a few days of abstinence, camels may drink as much as 100 litres in one go. In fact, on any lengthy journey, the well-being of the camel always took precedence over every other consideration. On arrival at a well, their thirst was satiated before the owners or herdsmen would attempt to drink; camels were allowed to forage for any available grazing even if the rider was in a hurry; camels were hand-fed on dates when there was no other food and they were given the last traces of water from the skins: the safe arrival of its rider depended entirely on the capabilities of his mount.

Traditionally, camel-herding was at its peak in winter-time when vast distances were covered in search of adequate grazing. The amount of time that any particular group devoted to this nomadic existence varied from tribe to tribe, depending mainly on whether they owned date gardens or not. During the day camels were left to roam,

At Wathiba Camel track (Vine)

herded by young men, returning at evening to the encampment. During these winter months, camels may last for six to seven months without drinking any water, provided there is sufficient grazing. During the summer, Bedouin travelled to wells as near as possible to grazing. Sometimes the wells are extremely bitter and the camels will only drink if their nostrils are closed by the herder. Sometimes the water in a well is so deep the camels cannot be left to drink by themselves; the water has to be drawn up in bags of skin and, since camels can drink enormous quantities in one go, watering a large herd during the summer can be a long hard haul. Today, the camel herdsman will probably be of Sudanese or Pakistani origin whilst the owner oversees the herding from a bright new four wheel-drive vehicle. But the camel is just the same, still commanding a tremendous amount of affection, respect and admiration from his owner. Quite naturally, locals take great care of their camels, and during severe weather conditions may extend water and shelter to them at their own temporary inconvenience and that of their families. A name is given to the calf as soon as it is born, frequently adding the tribal suffix to appellations such as 'Ghaseea, Afeera or Hamda. This love and respect for the camel is not confined to a rural setting: it is not unusual to see camel-pens attached to palatial residences in suburbia.

On occasions camels may wander far from their temporary home base, but disputes regarding ownership are avoided by branding. Camels are usually individually owned but since every Arab can identify his own animals in a herd, entire groups or even tribes can use the same brand-mark or **wasm**. Stories of lengthy unaccompanied treks and their eventual return home are legendary: a group of camels transported 1,600 kilometres from home-base eventually arrived back there, whilst it has also been reported that a camel covered two hundred kilometres in order to become reunited with its mate. Herds are guarded during the rutting season, great care is taken at that stage to control which animals are kept together. Most herds will have one rutting male with twenty to thirty females; the male or leading female is tethered, keeping the camels close by. Courtship and mating generally occurs from December to March, the males becoming extremely aggressive, grinding their teeth, salivating and blowing the dulaa or skin bladder out of their mouths. Calves are born from January to March, and remain with their mothers until about four years old. Only the female calves are raised, with the exception of a few stallions; male calves are slaughtered for special occasions. Many bedouin families in the Abu Dhabi region owned extensive flocks of sheep and goats along with their herds of

Dates: basic mainstay of the traditional economy. (Kay)

camels, as did semi-settled communities in more fertile zones who didn't have to journey so far afield for grazing. Donkeys also proved useful for carrying water and as pack-animals in general in agricultural areas.

To the Bedouin camels are almost sacred. Their importance was recently emphasised by a local who recalled: "They also defended us against attackers: we used to ride for two to three months in order to drive away marauders". Large convoys of camels crossed the desert from Abu Dhabi, Al Ain and Dubai, carrying firewood, charcoal, agricultural products and livestock to the towns and returning with much needed supplies to the desert camp or small villages. Camels transported whole families and their belongings from the humid coast to summer activities in the cooler oases. Camels were also the main means of transport for pilgrims visiting Mecca on the Haj. One Bedouin, recently reminiscing on this period, told of departing from Al Ain and riding for twenty-five days before arriving at Al Hasa in Saudi Arabia, an epic journey across the sands.

No one can deny that the life of the Bedouin has changed dramatically in recent years: the much lauded but extremely arduous nomadic existence has been abandoned for the comfort of settled houses in towns and villages, but animals, and especially the camel, still play a central role in this new lifestyle.

Date-cultivation

Dates have been the staple diet of the inhabitants of the UAE territory for many thousands of years, the date palm not only providing nourishment for the human population but, in many cases, fodder for their animals, as well as palm fronds to construct **barasti** dwellings and even weave small boats. The leaves of date palms were also used to make fans, baskets, bags, food trays and other useful items. The fibrous bark from the base of the tree provided material for ropes and stuffing for mattresses and camel saddles. Date palms can be grown from seed, but the usual way of obtaining a new tree is by transplanting a shoot sprouting from the base of a mature tree: if well watered, such new plants may bear fruit after three years. Because only female date palms bear fruit, very few male trees are planted in a garden. As a result pollen must be transferred by hand and not left to insects or the wind for dispersal. The date palm, if left to its own devices will form a bush, but active pruning encourages the cultivated plant to form a tree; the stumps of the branches lopped in pursuit of height forming convenient footholds for pollinators and harvesters. The height of the tree, as also the quality of its fruit depends to a great extent on the variety of palm, but is also deeply influenced by the amount of water available to irrigate the plants. Even when plenty of water is on hand for irrigation, the dates are harvested before they are entirely ripe to prevent dehydration. Most are consumed fresh but can be preserved for later use by boiling. The midsummer date harvest was an occasion for socialising as well as hard work, giving many families an opportunity to enjoy the relatively cool and green environs of the oases.

The date gardens in the scattered, crescent-shaped Liwa oasis and other desert locations survived with a little irrigation from wells. Only the youngest date palms received water on a regular basis, the liquid transported by hand from well to plant. The roots of date trees, cultivated without an irrigation system, grow vertically rather than horizontally, soon reaching the water table which is close to the surface in the Liwa and other small desert oases. Only certain types of date palm, producing smaller and less plentiful fruit, can thrive in these difficult conditions. Because of the scarcity of water and poor top-soil rendered even more infertile by drifting sand, it was not possible to engage in any other agricultural activity. However, in recent years some farmers in the Liwa have started to extend and diversify using modern materials and techniques.

Date-cultivation and more generalised agricultural activity benefited in other oases from the **falaj** system of irrigation. Falajes (Arabic plural is **aflaj**), still in use to this day, constitute an ingenious irrigation network, reputed to have its origins in the Persian Qanat system. In the UAE they distribute underground water brought close to the surface by artesian wells on the plains below the Hajar mountains; the life-giving liquid flows through gently sloping tunnels to agricultural areas, often over distances of up to 35 kilometres or more, emerging eventually into open channels whose flow is directed and regulated. In fact there are two types of **falaj** in the UAE: **dawoudi** and **ghaili.** The former, common to the lower-lying oases of Al Ain, Daid or Mazyad is fed by an abundant spring of underground water, running day and night all year round unless blocked by debris; whereas the **ghaili,** found in the upper reaches of the wadis, has a much less dependable source in the streams running through the gravel of the wadi beds, often just below the surface. To construct a **falaj,** vertical shafts were dug down at varying intervals, providing air for the excavators and facilitating the removal of soil and rock. Excavation took place between each shaft, piles of debris, like molehills, gradually accumulating beside the entrance. These shafts often remained in place to allow for maintenance and for the removal of water by bucket or pump. Underground tunnels were usually around five feet square, just large enough for man or boy to work in. On completion of the canal, the water source was then allowed to flow through the length of the **falaj,** its course depending on the slope of the ground surface and the depth of the water being tapped: evaporation was obviously minimised by the enclosed nature of the structure. Extremely well constructed and ingeniously built, many of the old systems, probably originating in pre-Islamic times, were allowed to become dilapidated but have now been patiently restored, modern pumping techniques often replacing the old artesian wells. The **falaj** was used to irrigate a number of gardens, a single channel dividing into several channels of equal width. Passing under the mud-brick walls enclosing the individual gardens, each channel further divides into shallow trenches carrying the water in different directions to the small date-palm holdings. The sharing of this precious resource was supervised by an **arif** or water superintendent, who blocked one of the channels with a stone slab and opened another.

The main water supply at Al Ain, a centre for agricultural development since time immemorial, comes from an aquifer fed by rain off the nearby mountain range. One of the oldest **aflaj** exists in and around Al Ain which obtained its name from the Arabic word "spring" or Ain. Here there is still an **arif** who, declaring that the **aflaj** were as old as the Prophet Suleiman bin Dawood (Solomon the son of David), explained the timing system used to apportion the water. On the basis of the '**bada**' made up of 12 hours, each **bada** comprising 24 **sudas**, each **suda** allowing a flow for 30 minutes, the Arif decides with the aid of a sundial or by monitoring the position of stars in the sky just when each division was completed. Shares in the irrigation rotation were divided equally, at least in principle, amongst individual farmers e.g. bada al Mualla, bada Saqr, bada al Nasser etc, all contributing to the cost of its upkeep by the payment of a fixed sum (a **masha**). A **bada** could also be owned or inherited by one family who would either use it, lease or sell it. Some farmers did not use all their **bada** at once, but received it in **suduses;** some with larger gardens requiring more water could buy extra irrigation time, the **arif** using this money to pay wages and repair the **falaj.**

Besides their crucial role in dividing and allocating the suduses fairly, **arifs** also had other uses. Before a **falaj** system was constructed, they conducted a survey to find out whether a likely source did in fact have underground water. They also settled local disputes over irrigation rights amongst the owners of date palm gardens, with one **arif** controlling the water supply for as many as 80 gardens, in return for which he was entitled to one **bada** of irrigation either for his own use or for resale. In Al Ain the **arif** claims he is a farmer at heart: a much respected leader and arbitrator he is still called upon to assist the municipality's water engineers, his advice and knowledge of the **aflaj** being highly valued. In 1950 he was entrusted with the task of sinking new wells for the **falaj**, "al Sarrouj". Now an old man, he is pleased to see that today 11 million gallons of water a day are produced from the **aflaj** around Al Ain. But the dramatic increase in water consumption has however strained these ancient systems and although, in the past, there was enough water provided to sustain villages and farms, this is no longer the case. Traditionally, **falaj**-irrigated gardens supported other plants besides date palms. Oranges, lemons and limes were the most common trees, but mangoes, figs, mulberries, bananas and pomegranates seemed to thrive also. Some seasonal crops such as lucerne used for cattle-feed, cotton, wheat and barley grew underneath the trees, as did a variety of vegetables like water-melons, sweet potatoes, beans, garlic and onions. The area of ground under cultivation and the variety of crops planted has changed radically with the introduction of modern technology.

Despite the rapid construction of desalination plants, reservoirs and dams, drought in the mid 1980's coupled with the mushrooming of highly innovative, agricultural complexes and horticultural projects has caused the water table to drop at an alarming rate. However it is interesting to note that, even though in some cases the use of **aflaj** increased salinity levels, the majority of experts believe that the redevelopment of many of the old neglected irrigation channels will help to conserve water supplies. Consequently, UNESCO who are studying ways to improve this traditional method of watering in Arab countries, say that there is a good chance of maximising the old system with modern techniques.

Pearling

Pearling, an age-old industry, was the economic bulwark of the population along the southern Gulf littoral in the last century, allowing many groups depending on this valuable resource to flourish and acquire a settled status. Pearling continued to be a vitally important source of wealth right up to the early 1930's when this lucrative trade, already devastated by the Japanese introduction of the cultured pearl, was deeply affected by a decrease in demand due to economic depression in Europe and America. The extent of pearling activity in the Gulf in its heyday is well illustrated by Lorimer's calculation that, at its peak, over 1,200 pearling boats operated out of the Trucial States, each carrying an average crew of about 18 men. This meant that during the summer most able-bodied men, numbering more than 22,000, were absent on the pearl banks. The average annual value of pearls exported from the Gulf at the turn of the century was estimated at £1,434,399 and £30,439 was earned from the export of mother-of-pearl.

Pearling was not merely a trade or a means of subsistence but an entirely integrated social system, leaving a rich heritage of traditions to be enjoyed by an indigenous population who are now benefiting from the security engendered by oil revenues after centuries of hardship. The pearl banks near the southern shores of the Gulf were not the particular domain of any individual shaikdom, but were open to all pearling boats from Arab ports. The notion that these pearl banks belonged to the Arabs of the southern Gulf was and still is deeply ingrained: attempts by foreigners to exploit the resources by means of modern diving equipment have been thwarted in the last century and right up to the present time.

Ghaus (literally diving) is the general Arabic term used to denote the pearl fishery and all the classes that take part in the operations are included under the common denomination **ghawawis.** The method used in harvesting the pearl oyster (in fact three separate species of oyster, occupying different habitats, secrete the nacreous material required to form the precious pearl) was much the same throughout the region and probably had not altered radically in thousands of years. An 'admiral', appointed by the ruler in each port, set the date for sailing to and from the pearling banks. All the boats from the same port under the authority of one sheikh departed for the main summer harvest at the beginning of June in one great picturesque swoop of sail, and returned to port together, approximately 120 days later, towards the end of September. The graceful Arab vessels collectively known as dhows were employed as pearling boats, mostly **sambuks** but **jalibuts**, **batils**, **bagqarahs**, and **shu'ais** also had a place in the industry. Depending on the preference or particular strategy of the captain, a pearling boat might anchor for the entire season at one pearl bank or move from bank to bank. Short trips were made to ports such as Dalma for the renewal of drinking-water, rice, dates, coffee and tobacco.

The normal complement of crew for the average pearling vessel was 18–20; 8 divers or **ghasah** (sing. **ghais**), 10 haulers **siyub** (sing. **saib**) and an apprentice **walaid** (pl. **aulad**) who fished, cooked, cleaned and took care of the coffee. A **nahham** was only employed on the larger boats, to coordinate the

Fishing boat, loaded with fish traps, creates a pleasing silhouette against the darkening sky. (Vine)

Hauling seine nets on the east coast. Large shoals of sardines and anchovies are caught by this method. (Kay)

evocative rhythmical chants used to ease rigorous tasks on board. The captain (**nukhada**) chose the location of the dive and also took control of the sale of the catch.

Despite much nostalgic reflection on the communal spirit encountered in pearling, there is no doubt that life was extremely hard for the average diver who was often deeply in debt to the owner of the boat. Diving commenced about an hour after sunrise, the divers having breakfasted lightly on coffee and dates, and proceeded right through until an hour before sunset, except for prayers and sometimes coffee and a short rest at midday. The hard-working diver, nose pegged with clips of turtle shell (**ftam**) and ears plugged by wax, plummeted to the bottom aided by a stone (**hajar**) attached to his foot which was subsequently pulled up by his attendant hauler on board ship. Fingers protected by leather caps (**khabt**), he quickly filled an attached basket (**diyyin**) with as many shells as possible, finally signalling by a tug on his rope that he needed to be hauled to the surface. The diver rested in the water after his arduous task, holding onto his rope in characteristic repose, while his basket was being emptied; but it wasn't long before he was again descending to the deep. After an evening meal of fish and rice, complemented by dates and coffee, the crew attempted to settle down for the night on board the crowded deck to avail of the sea breezes that alleviate the dreadful heat and humidity. It wasn't until early morning that the pile of oyster shells were opened to reveal the day's catch. This all took place under the watchful eye of the captain who took a record of any particularly big pearls that might be sold individually.

Some **nukhada** sold the season's catch to a **tawwash** who visited the pearl banks from time to time while the diving was in progress, some made direct contact with wholesale pearl merchants (**tujar**) whilst others contracted with a financier at a prearranged price. The wholesaler arranged for the sale of the pearls and mother-of-pearl to Indian pearl merchants present for the lucrative season. Although pearl-gathering techniques were more or less the same throughout the UAE, disparities arose in the structuring of the industry because of the sociological differences between the Abu Dhabi pearling community and those of other sheikdoms in the area. The term **ikhluwi** indicated a co-operative system in which the crew and the **nukhada** shared all the net profit of the season, distributed in a set manner depending on the type of work each individual performed. **Amil** denoted a financing method whereby the boat was owned and fitted out by an entrepreneur who was entitled to a major part of the proceeds at the end of the season, leaving the rest to be divided among the crew. However, the **Amil**, a system originally confined to shaikdoms other than that of Abu Dhabi, was widely applicable at the end of the century. It originally arose because pearlers, who belonged to different tribes and did not own date gardens, were not in a position to supply a pearling boat with the necessities so readily available to those closely related tribal groups that did

Rich harvest at Sha'am, Ras Al Khaimah. (Vine)

have these assets. However when surplus funds became available as the market for pearls expanded, the life of the versatile Abu Dhabi tribesmen took on a more specialised nature. Whereas before the tribal pearling cooperative earned only enough to subsist, suddenly there was excess money available. Some utilised their share to buy more camels, others added to their date gardens, both groups paying labourers to take care of their property in their absence. Still others invested in the pearling industry so that, eventually, most boats were owned by individuals who finally took up residence in Abu Dhabi in the winter, living off their pearl earnings. Eventually entrepreneurs dominated the industry in Abu Dhabi, as they had already done for some time in other areas. The specialisation that evolved in these pearling communities meant that much of the egalitarian nature of the tribal society was replaced by a wage-earning system. This degree of specialisation was to be the downfall of these businessmen and indeed all those who depended on the pearling industry. Franke Heard-Bey remarks that "*by contrast, the way of life of the tribal population in Abu Dhabi was not affected so radically by the decline of the pearling industry, because the families who had retained their roots in the desert concentrated again on utilising its resources.*"

Fishing

The fishing industry was overshadowed by the more lucrative and romantic pearling trade, but it has managed to emerge into the 1980's in a better shape than the other traditional occupations we have already discussed. Coastal fishing communities still successfully exploit fishery resources found off the 540 kilometres of Gulf coastline in the possession of the UAE. The east coast, adjoining the Gulf of Oman, is blessed with long curving beaches and sandy bays interrupted only by rocky outcrops where the bare Hajar mountains stretch into the sea. The western coast, on the other hand, has much shallow water close to the shore, as well

A fisherman rests on the bowsprit of his fishing boat. (Vine)

Domed fish traps piled high on a fishing craft. (Vine)

as islands, sandbanks, lagoons, reefs and tidal channels rendering conditions extremely difficult for navigation except for those very familiar with the area. Fishing continues to be a worthwhile occupation on both coasts. The southern Gulf is particularly productive during September to March, when rich, cooler, less saline waters from the Indian Ocean flow through the Straits of Hormuz into the lower Gulf, bringing with them large numbers of pelagic fish. The east coast benefits considerably from a constant upwelling of deep oceanic water facilitating the growth of plankton. Since inshore waters are so rich, deep sea fishing has not been developed to any great extent. Trawling for demersal fish is also not worthwhile because the continental shelf is narrow and the grounds are not suitable. Fresh fish, available at local fish souks for those that cannot fish, was often the only source of protein for the indigenous coastal population. Sun-dried fish was also a valuable food source for people inland, as well as fodder for animals and fertiliser (usually sardines) for crops. Because of the seasonal and part-time nature of the fishing for many of its participants, it is difficult to estimate the exact number of fishermen that were involved. Some however did depend entirely on the sea for their living even after the decline of the pearling industry.

Because the sea and date gardens are in such close proximity on the east coast, and in Ras Al Khaimah, it was possible to easily combine fishing and agriculture. But, outside of these areas, the fertile oases are far removed from the fishing grounds, hindering any individual attempts to successfuly combine both occupations. Abu Dhabi, where the oases of Liwa and Al Ain are distant from the infertile shore and islands, illustrates the difficulties involved. Fishing and pearling eventually became the exclusive occupation of a small group of people in the sheikdom of Abu Dhabi. Some of Abu Dhabi's islands were permanently inhabited by Rumaithat and Qubaisat fishermen, both sub-sections of the Bani Yas. Fishing rights were rented from the Ruler: families who lived from fishing on the islands and on the coasts paid one-fifth of the catch to the main holder of the fishing rights. Such rights were held primarily by Rumaithat, but also by some of the Qubaisat, Al Bu Falash and Rawashid sections of the Bani Yas. Members of Manasir, Awamir or Al Murrah tribes rarely fished because few of them owned boats, but some did join the crew of pearling boats. Communal effort was not required for successful fishing off the coast of Abu Dhabi as was necessary in the pearling industry.

Age-old methods of harvesting the sea are still very much in evidence even if, as in the other traditional occupation, the nationality of the personnel involved has changed to a certain degree. Frequently, two nets (**masakir**) anchored to a central pole are set across the mouth of a small creek, or along the beach, at high tide to trap the fish as the waters ebb. Sometimes, observing a shoal of fish in shallow water, a solitary fisherman fastens one end of his net to a pole on the shore (**makhir**) and, using a dug-out, draws the opposite end of

Launching a **shashah**, a palm frond canoe of ancient design on the east coast. (Kay)

the weighted net in a wide semi-circle to a point further up the shore. As it is pulled inwards, the encircled shoal swim for an opening in the net behind which is a fish trap. A similar method (**idfarah**) without the trap is worked by two or three people, one holding the middle of the net with his feet whilst the others haul. Long seine-nets are still set parallel to the shore , both sides being drawn in at once, entrapping sparkling shoals of silver sardines and other fish which are thrown up for collection by the women and children on the beach; weighted cast-nets are flung in graceful sharp-wristed movements by fishermen stalking the shallows; and semi-spherical, wire fish-traps (**qarqur**), originally constructed from palm-fronds, are also set on the bottom. Wooden rowing boats, holding about ten people, were sometimes used for fishing; east-coast fishermen still employ small frail craft known as **shashahs** to surmount the surf; larger wooden surf boats (**amlah**), capable of accommodating up to 40 crew, originally fitted with sails and oars but now probably motorised as well, are used to set very long beach seines. To maximise on the potential of these artisanal fisheries, and to supplement fresh produce on the UAE market, the government has supplied local fishermen with modern fibre-glass boats equipped with out-board engines and has improved harbour facilities along the coast.

Large **boum** in Sharjah creek. (Kay)

Hand-tools are still used for much of the construction work involved in local boat-building. (Vine)

Boat-building

When pearling was at its climax, the most important manufacturing industry of the southern Gulf was boat-building. But, surprisingly, the construction of dhows is still very much a living tradition in the Emirates with at least as many traditional craft being constructed now as at the beginning of the century. At that time Umm Al Quwain was an important boat-building centre; about 20 boats were built there per year while only approximately 10 were fashioned in Dubai. Today Ajman has the largest dhow building yard on the coast. Teak (**saj**) for planking, and for the keel, stem, stern and masts of the larger boats has traditionally been imported from India; **mit** for the naturally grown crooks used to form ribs and knees from India, Somalia, Iran, and Iraq; rope from Zanzibar and the sail canvas from Bahrain or Kuwait, although some was made locally. Mango was also imported from India to make the smaller boats and dug-outs (**huri**). Only the **shashah,** built usually by its user, was made entirely from parts of the local date palm.

The dhow shipyards in the Emirates nurture this ancient boat-building tradition, using the same basic materials and tools to fashion elegant craft. Shell construction involving the fitting of planks first and ribs later is the usual system employed in dhow construction, contrasting with the European method of forming a skeleton of ribs prior to planking. Boats are all carvel-built with planks laid edge to edge: hundreds, sometimes thousands of holes are hand-drilled to avoid splitting the wood and long thin nails, wrapped in oiled fibre, are driven through to secure the planks to the frames. All the construction work is carried out without the aid of plans and drawings, measurements being made solely by eye and experience; templates are, however, used to shape the hull planking. Although it appears that accuracy depends solely on the instinct of the boat-builders, in fact a highly experienced master-craftsman (**ustadh**) usually oversees the calculations. The tools used in building boats, from the smallest to the largest, are very simple , hammer, saw, adze, bow-drill, chisel, plane and caulking iron are, amazingly, all that is required to produce such a sophisticated and graceful end-product. The building of a large vessel could take anything up to ten months, while a smaller one—a **shu'ai** for instance—would be finished in one to four months.

Construction of Arab craft, in the pre-Portuguese era differed somewhat from the modern form. Three distinctive features epitomised the dhows of this early period: coconut fibre, rather

The boat-building yards of Abu Dhabi are a haven of traditionalism where sounds of hammering, sawing and planing mingle to create a sense of timelessness. (Vine)

than nails was used to sew the planks of the hull together; the hull shape was double-ended as opposed to square-sterned; and the sails had a fore- and aft- rather than square-rigged arrangement. All three features can be found on the east coast but, except in the Omani sewn **sambuk**, never in the one boat. The Portuguese introduced new concepts into the art of ship-building in the Arab world; European influence over the centuries finally culminating in a wide selection of dhows with square sterns, but the double-ended form persists in the **boum** and **badan**, among others. Although the lateen sail remained unchanged, the nailing of planks together supplanted the less robust method of sewing.

Different types of vessel falling under the collective western title of dhow are individually named according to their particular hull shape. **Baghlah**, **boum**, **sambuk**, **shu'ai**, **batil**, **bagqarah** and **jalibut** and, to a lesser extent, the **huri** and **shashah** were all common in the Gulf at one stage or another. Varieties on which it is inconvenient or impossible to modify hulls to accommodate engines have, by and large, fallen into disuse and are no longer being built except for museum purposes. Sterns of all suitable types have been adapted and ribs extended to make way for modern engines and outboard motors are now fitted on large numbers of dug-outs or **huris** and other fishing craft. Sometimes, however, one can spot a new functional and streamlined hull form, not corresponding to any traditional classification, developed specifically to accommodate an engine.

The double-ended **boum** is now the largest of all Arab vessels in the Gulf, attaining a length anywhere between 50 to 120 ft. Easily distinguishable by its high, straight stem-post, built out into a kind of planked bowsprit decorated with a simple design in black and white, it has superceded the ornately decorated square-sterned, high-pooped **baghlah** as a trading vessel. The **boum** can be seen in great numbers jostling for space at the quays of Dubai, laden with an eclectic selection of goods from many different countries. The **sambuk**, boasting an infinite variety of sizes, used to be one of the most common Arab vessels of the Gulf and is still very much in evidence. A low curved, scimitar-shaped stem piece and high square stern lend elegance and grace to the lines of this useful boat. The length of the stem piece underwater and the resulting short keel allowed for easy manoeuvrability on the sand banks, making this a most popular pearling vessel but it was, and still is, used for trading and fishing purposes. **Shu'ai**, basically small **sambuks**, rarely over 15 tons, but sporting a straight as opposed to curved stem piece are commonly used as fishing vessels. **Shashah**, on the other hand, are a totally different class of craft needing little skill and experience to build. Small (about 10 ft.) and basic, they are made of date

Planks for boat-building at Abu Dhabi's boat yards are cut from huge tree trunks using this ancient looking band-saw. (Vine)

The dhow building area at Abu Dhabi is conveniently adjacent to deep-water. It is one of the best places in the entire Gulf to observe traditional craft being built. (Vine)

palm sticks tied with coir to form a point at bow and stern. Palm bark, coconut fibre and the bulbous ends of palm branches, packed into the bottom of the boat under a makeshift decking, lend buoyancy so that the boat lies flat on the water like a raft. Polystyrene is now favoured as a method of keeping afloat and the substitution of nylon thread for coir has given greater strength to these fragile but flexible craft. It is precisely this flexibility that enables the **shashah** to withstand the pounding surf common on the Batinah coast where they prove so popular.

The traditional boat-building yards of Abu Dhabi, ranged against a silhouetted back-drop of shining skyscrapers, provide the visitor with a unique image of sea-faring past linked to technologically orientated present. At the Al Bhutin boat factory boat owners arrive by Mercedes, Cadillac and Rolls Royce, pulling up alongside airconditioned wooden shacks on the sand-spit between sea and creek. Everything necessary for the boat-building and fishing industry is fabricated here. Imported teak planks are cut on ancient band saws; iron nails forged at a makeshift foundry; anchors, fish traps and boats of every description take shape under the careful eye of skilled craftsmen. A very large **jalibut**, under construction for Shaikh Zayed, dwarfed the other traditional craft when I last visited the yard. The warm dry smell of wood shavings overwhelmed by the pungent aroma of linseed oil permeates the nostrils as one observes the unhurried movements of fishing boats entering and leaving the area; some lie at anchor with the crew relaxing at cards on the after-deck or perhaps eating, crouched around a communal tray. Rangy cats hide amongst the piled planks, hoping to pounce on fallen scraps; seagulls screech, wheeling above the industrious scene whilst a gentle breeze ruffles the calm sea. Even the rueful presence of a few fibreglass fishing boats, donated by the government, only underlines the defiantly persistent stance boat-building has made against the encroachment of modernity.

TRADITIONAL HANDICRAFTS

Most crafts were associated with traditional occupations or the provision of household objects and were limited by the range of materials available locally and the lack of permanence in the lifestyle of the people. Metal working, involving the manufacture of silver, gold and copper objects as well as jewellery, is a very old tradition in the UAE. We have already spoken of the copper-crafting utensils found in tombs of the 3rd millenium BC civilisation of Umm an Nar and the gold objects discovered in the early 2nd millenium

Traditional coffee pots were made of copper or brass. (Kay)

tombs at Qatarra. Silver and gold jewellery retained its popularity throughout the ages, as the region consolidated its role as a trading link between many different cultures, each bringing their influence to bear on design and manufacture. Craftsmen in the souks of Sharjah, Dubai and Ras Al Khaimah transformed silver into heavy bedouin jewellery, intricate silver boxes, buttons, decorations on knife handles and scabbards, hubble-bubbles and many other everyday items. Gold was also used and has, in recent times, usurped the prominent role silver played in metal crafting.

Household utensils were invariably made of copper including cooking pans, distinctive coffee pots, beakers, dishes and incense burners. Sometimes copper vessels were plated for protection with other metals such as lead and aluminium. Tools were also made of copper, as were nails, but iron eventually proved more enduring in this field although household utensils continued to be made from copper and clay pottery predominated prior to the advent of plastic.

Pottery vessels have been used in the territory of the UAE for thousands of years: grave goods from the 3rd millennium tombs of the Umm an Nar culture included clay pots of very sophisticated manufacture. In more recent times some

Small metal boxes were locally made. (Kay)

Swords, guns and daggers were often decorated with repousse silver-work, as on this fine sword sheath. (Kay)

household pottery, such as big water storage jars and large earthenware cooking pots, were imported from Iran. Other pottery items came from further afield, but there is also reasonably good clay near Ras Al Khaimah and around Al Ain from which storage jars, round bottomed water jugs which kept water cool through evaporation, and conical pottery drinking beakers, but especially incense burners were made. These pottery objects were sold in the local markets.

Various other items were manufactured for domestic use from the materials that were at hand. Camel or goat hides were turned into waterbags and other containers as well as sandals to protect against the burning sand. Under normal circumstances, none of these items were made for sale but for the use of the maker or members of his family and tribe.

Most of the cloth used by the population of the UAE was not woven locally but imported from India and other countries. Al Ain, Ras Al Khaimah, and possibly some other major settlements had professional weavers who sold their product in the local souqs. Women wove items such as tents from goat hair and sheep wool as they were required by the family.

Basic looms have been set up at the Abu Dhabi Handicraft Centre organised by the Ministry of Labour and Social Affairs with the support of Sheikha Fatima bint Mubarak, wife of the UAE President, Sheikh Zayed bin Sultan Al Nahyan, to encourage the preservation of handicrafts in the Emirates. Other crafts practised under the auspices of the Handicraft Centre are palmfibre braiding and tallis making. Palmfibre is one of the few natural resources available and no equipment

A close-up of a rug being woven at the Handicraft Centre in Abu Dhabi. (Vine)

is required to practise this art. Some dyeing of fibres is carried out to create a particular pattern when blended with the natural material. Women sitting on the floor, wetting their hands at intervals to smooth the material, create a variety of useful objects such as floor-mats and prayer-mats, food covers, bags, baskets and fans among others. Tallis making is still a very vibrant craft in the UAE since it is used extensively in the decoration of traditional dress. Using a small pillow resting on a stand **(kajouda)** women, with tremendous dexterity, weave these long strips of braid from cotton, gold and silver threads into exquisite patterns.

Close-up of intricate design on a rug still on the loom at the Handicraft Centre, Abu Dhabi. (Vine)

Rich vibrant colours, seen here in the rug under manufacture at the Women's Handicraft Centre and the dress of its maker, traditionally provided a welcome contrast to the bleakness of the sandy desert. (Vine)

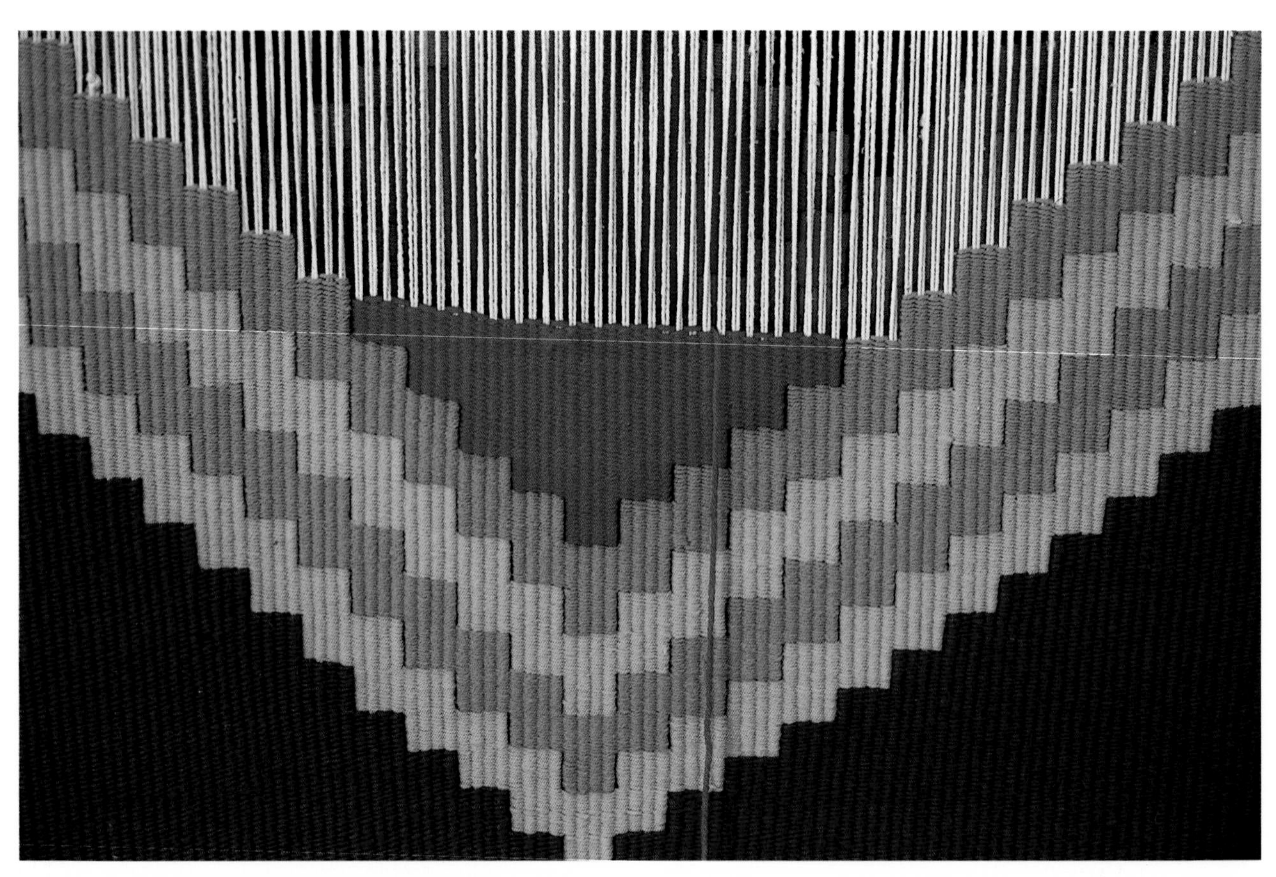

Rug-weaving in Women's Handicraft Centre, Abu Dhabi. (Vine)

Typical geometric design on rug woven in traditional manner. (Vine)

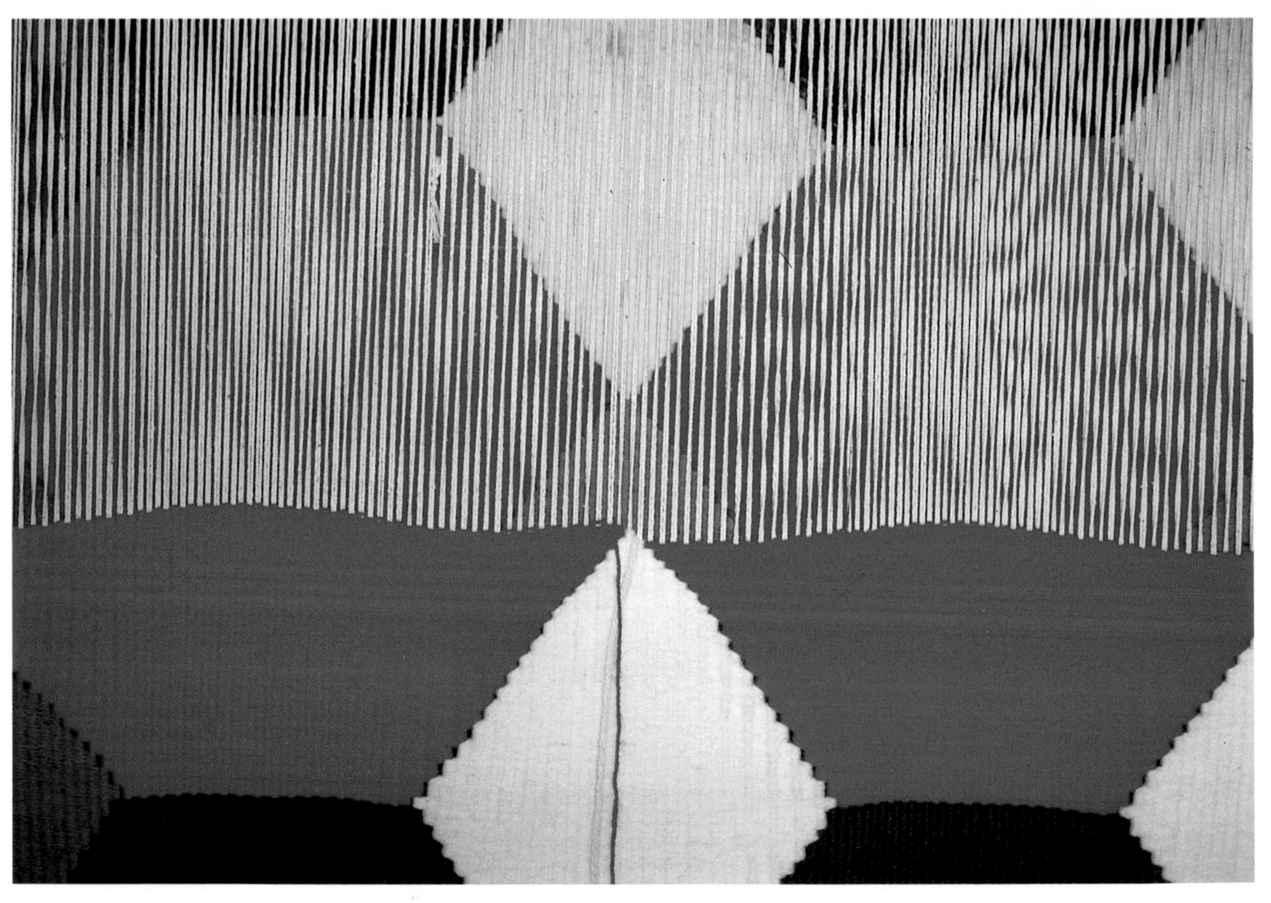

Tallis work used to embellish traditional dress in the UAE. (Vine)

Old traditional-style rug in Abu Dhabi. (Vine)

Dyed strands mingle with natural palmfibres to create a subtle pattern. (Vine)

Palmfibre braiding at the Women's Handicraft Centre, Abu Dhabi. (Vine)

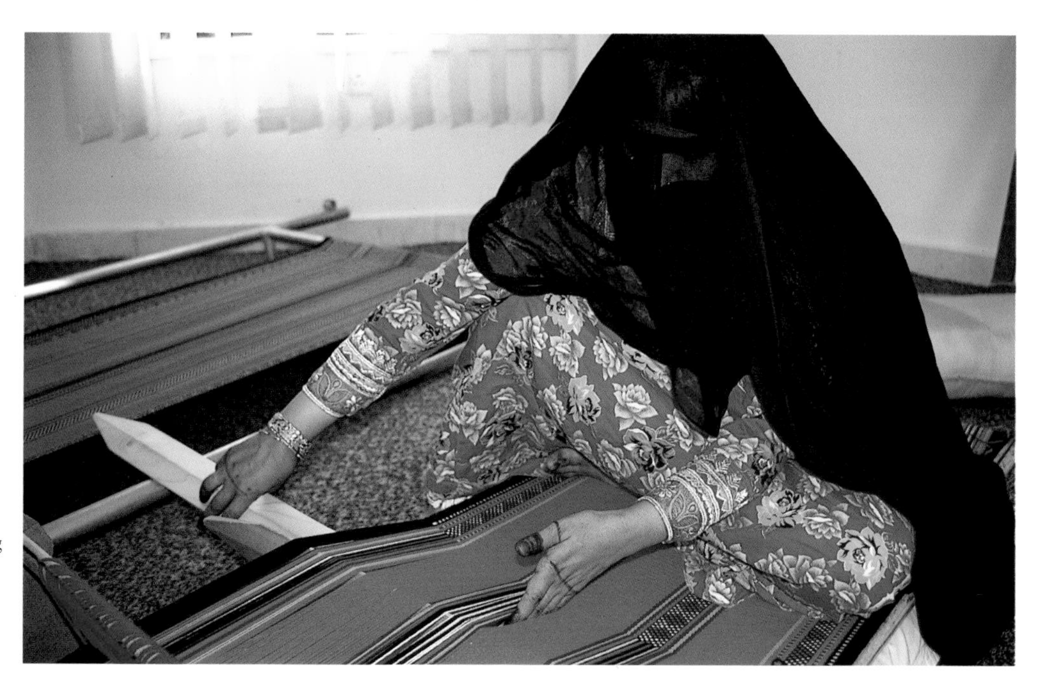
Bedouin woman weaving a colourful rug on a simple loom at the Handicraft Centre, Abu Dhabi. (Vine)

At Wathiba Camel track (Vine)

TRADITIONAL SPORTS

Life wasn't entirely spent in pursuit of sustenance; time was also allotted to sporting activities and these traditional past-times are now enjoying a welcome revival.

Camel-racing

We have heard how much the Bedouin loved, respected and admired his camel, it is not so surprising then that they wished to pit their best beasts in informal camel-races. This ancient sport has been revived with so much enthusiasm in recent years that, over and above informal desert tracks, there are now quite a few official ones: a large ten kilometre .track on the Al Ain road, about forty-five kilometres from Abu Dhabi city; at Al Ain itself; at Dubai and Umm Al Quwain. Certain slender, finely-formed breeds such as the white or golden '**Anafi**' and the brown or black '**Boushari**' are more suitable for racing. Camel-training commences at about six months, entrance for official races beginning at about three years. Racing life, for the male at least, ends at about ten, but the female may race until she is at least twenty years. As in all racing animals, exercise, in the form of walking and galloping, and diet are particularly important: racing camels are usually fed on oats, bran, dates and cows milk but quantities are much reduced shortly before the race itself. The weight of the jockey is also crucial to the success of the venture, so very young boys, sometimes no more than six years of age, are used as mounts, riding either perched on the camel's hump or, in bedouin style, behind.

Camel-races, usually held early on Fridays or on national holidays, provide visitors with a

A diminutive rider relaxes before the race leaning on his camel. (Vine)

Smart four-wheel drive vehicles provide an unusual background for more traditional desert transport. (Vine)

unique opportunity to observe traditionally-clad local people in harmony with their surroundings. Away from the sophistication of the viewing stand and the race-track, the competitors and their handlers gather to prepare themselves and their mounts for the race. Apart from the serious aspect of competing , the occasion is a social one where many camel riders meet with friends whom they may not have seen for a considerable period. At a time when the UAE is developing into a modern, efficient country, there are relatively few opportunities to experience such valued glimpses of the past.

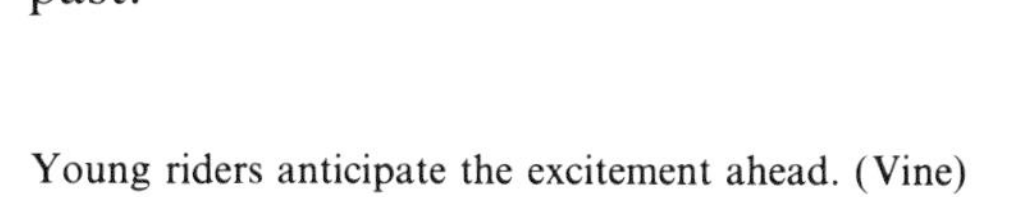

Young riders anticipate the excitement ahead. (Vine)

Camels en route to starting line. (Vine)

At Wathiba Camel track (Vine)

Bedu boy at camel races. (Vine)

Falconry

Falconry, an integral part of desert life, practised originally for purely practical reasons, i.e. the necessity to supplement a meagre diet of dates, milk and bread, developed into a major sport enjoyed by rich and poor alike. Hunting parties originally pursued their quarry on horseback or camel but powerful four wheel-drive vehicles are fast replacing traditional modes of transport. It is difficult to supplant the captivating image of a desert horseman, arm outstretched to support a motionless bird of prey; man, bird and horse at one in dignity and bearing, with the lurching, fume-filled presence of the cross-country truck.

The Saker (*Falco cherruq*), imported from other Middle Eastern countries, and the Peregrine (*Falco peregrinus*), are the two main species used for hunting in the Emirates, the former being the most popular since it is well suited to desert hawking. The female Saker (**al hurr**), larger and more powerful is utilised more frequently than the male (**garmoush**). Sakers, brave, patient hunters with keen eyesight, take naturally to Houbara, their primary quarry. They are less fussy feeders and more able to cope with the stress and rigours of

The falcon is hooded until released in flight to pursue her prey. (Kay)

Horse-Racing

The Arab horse is a legendary creature invoking images of grace stamina and strength, silken mane and tail streaming as it flies across the sand. The most ancient of all tamed horses, it has a distinctive appearance with a short back, small head showing a concave profile, large intelligent eyes and tail carried high. All Thoroughbred racehorses are descended from three Arabian stallions, and, having been bred for centuries to win races, these are now the swiftest of all horses but cannot rival the smaller, pure-bred Arab for endurance. The Arab's fame has spread throughout the world where it is cherished and admired not only as a truly valued breed but as a means to lighten and improve heavier types. This beautiful animal is no less cherished on its home territory. Bedu have bred the Arab horse with dedication over the centuries, particularly as a fast and agile mount for battle, but horses were never widely used in the territory of the UAE, either for transport, agriculture or warfare. Much of the terrain is too soft and food and water too scarce to utilise these animals to their full potential. However the Arab horse was always prized and especially welcomed as a gift between sheikhs and nowadays both pure Arabians and Thoroughbreds are reared and raced in the UAE. Private races are held throughout the winter, Abu Dhabi and Umm Al Quwain being the leading centres.

A falconer and his bird in the desert near Dubai. (Kay)

camp life than the temperamental Peregrine whose brittle feathers tend to get damaged when struggling with Houbara. The female Peregrine (**shahin** or **bahri shahin**) is also preferred to the male (**shahin tiba**) for hunting purposes. The Lanner (*Falco biarmicus*), regarded as the beginner's hawk, was much favoured by the Bedu but has ceased to be so popular.

Wild falcons are trapped during their autumn migration and trained in readiness for the hunting season, beginning in late November. Both haggards or adult birds (**gernass**) and passagers, first year birds (**fahr**), are trained to hunt, the training period lasting up to three weeks. Some falcons are released in the spring when the hunting season has ended to continue on to their breeding grounds, although many are kept through the long hot summer for a further season of sport, but illness is always a high risk during the extreme heat. Captive-breeding is not a solution to these problems. Captive-bred birds often lack the instinct of the predator and therefore fail to perform as well as their wild counterparts. Over and above this difficulty, the young hatch in May or June facing into the stresses of the summer months and, since females are preferred for hunting purposes, male hatchlings pose a problem. Captive birds cannot be returned easily to the wild, especially those that are totally foreign to the local habitat as is the case of Australian Peregrines. Hybrid species, powerful and infertile, can also cause pressure on local species by competing aggressively for breeding areas.

Birds may be purchased from a trapper and are often received as gifts, but part of the traditional attraction of falconry was to catch one's own wild falcon. Each owner begins his training period by concentrating on getting to know his bird, frequently giving it an individual name. A soft leather hood (**al burqa**) is placed over the head and gathered together at the back with the leather traces. Slowly but surely the falcon learns to accept food from the trainer's hand, gradually becoming used to both the touch and sound of her trainer. During this learning process the falcon sits on a round wooden mushroom shaped movable block (**al wakr**) or on the trainer's hand which is protected from the sharp talons by a cylindrical carpet-covered cuff (**mangalah**), more common in the Emirates than a leather glove. The bird is held by a pair of jesses, usually braided cotton or nylon (**al sabbuq**) attached to a swivelled leash to allow the bird a certain freedom of movement.

When the falcon has become accustomed to its handler, the hood is removed so that visual contact can be established, a bond of dependence being slowly forged as the bird accepts food. Still leashed, the falcon is allowed to jump from the

wakr to the **mangalah,** at which time she is considered to have become tame and the next step of training is undertaken out in the desert, in the late afternoon or early evening. The hooded falcon remains perched on the hand of an assistant, attached by string to the jesses or the end of the leash while the trainer walks a short distance away. Turning towards the falcon he swings a lure, usually a pair of dried Houbara wings sewn together and tied to a fresh piece of meat, with which the bird is rewarded once she has downed the bait. On hearing the trainer call, the falcon is unhooded and immediately flies towards the familiar sound: the lure is lowered as the bird approaches so that she may bind to the lure just off the ground. As soon as the falcon swoops on the lure and brings it down, she is coaxed onto the trainer's hand for the expected reward of meat.

During initial training flights, the lure gives way to live pigeons, thrown into the air as the falcon is released. Gradually, during training, the distance the falcon is encouraged to fly increases up to several hundred metres. Patient training is well rewarded when the hunting season begins, the main prey being Houbara, Stone Curlew (**kiriwan**) or Hare (**arnab**). Excitement and expectancy coupled with sheer enjoyment of the chase are the predominant emotions as the quarry is sighted and the hood removed from the falcon. The chase begins. The stout dumpy Houbara (*Chlamydotis undulata macqueenii*) are strong expert fliers, twisting and turning at great speed, but a well-trained falcon can bring four or five bustards down during a single hunting session. It is the chase itself that impresses and excites, the prey no longer required to fill the larder. Both Sakers and Peregrines kill in the air and on the ground. The Peregrine in pursuit of prey flies very fast to get above its victim and then makes a sudden headlong dash, called a stoop, at tremendous speed. Although the Peregrine is extremely fast over short distances, the Saker has more stamina.

As the shadowy evening light descends, the hunting party clean their booty and, while it is cooking over the open fire, sit and discuss in a timeless fashion the day's chase, each extolling the skill and courage of their best falcon, arguing their victories and defeats of the day: a disparaging remark about a bird can reflect on the honour of the falconer. The pleasure of the hunt is shared equally by ruler, minister, merchant or tribesman, all experiencing companionship through a sport that has been a tradition amongst the Arab people for hundreds of years.

A very special facility has been created for falcons in Dubai, a luxury which was certainly not available to the tribal hunter. The Dubai Falcon Hospital, the only one of its kind in the UAE, has treated over 1500 falcons since it was first set up five years ago. The consulting veterinarian, a keen falconer himself, says that 90% of the species brought in to the hospital to be treated are Sakers and Peregrines captured while on their migration routes: the Kestrel is the only species of falcon that breeds in Dubai. The hospital, which receives patients from all over the Gulf, has an extremely busy schedule treating up to 15 birds a day. Fully equipped with an anaesthesia machine, a heart monitor, an X-ray room, twelve recuperating chambers and blood-testing laboratory, it is completely air-conditioned. Falcons in the Gulf suffer from a number of common diseases, all of which can be treated at the hospital. Pox is transmitted by mosquitoes; lead poisoning is caused by falcons eating prey shot by lead pellets; trichomoniasis or "frounce" (**jiddri**) results from the consumption of stomach and throat of infected pigeons; aspergillosis arises through the inhalation of fungus spores which attack the lungs; and coccidiosis, is a parasitic disease affecting the intestines, causing loss of weight and diarrhoea. Another falcon ailment treated at the hospital is "bumble foot", or punctured feet, caused through standing on a hard surface for a long periods of time or through vitamin A deficiency; sometimes this can also arise because of self-injury inflicted by the long talons.

Peregrines are particularly susceptible to insecticides which, on absorption, can disrupt reproduction by weakening the eggshell, causing it to break before hatching. World populations of Peregrines suffered extensively shortly after the Second World War from the widespread use of DDT which has now been banned in most countries, although happily, numbers have now risen again to a respectable level. A certain amount of tension exists between falconers and conservationists who claim that the sport is responsible for the decline in the Houbara Bustard population, while falconers argue that they are even more concerned than conservationists to preserve their chief quarry. Over and above the sport of falconry, hunting with modern vehicles to penetrate the remote habitat of the bustard and the accuracy of powerful modern shotguns has meant that stocks have been severely depleted.

In fact very few Houbara now breed in the wild in the UAE. However, a few hundred visitors arrive from early October and may stay until March when they return to their breeding grounds in the southern steppes of Russia and western Mongolia. There is no doubt that without Houbara or any other suitable prey, falconry will eventually become a thing of the past. Houbara are particularly susceptible to environmental change because of their delayed maturity, low fertility and long lifespan. While it would not be true to say that traditional hawking is solely responsible for the sudden decline in Houbara populations, unless present efforts to protect the breeding grounds of Houbara and other species are continued and intensified, the future availability of wild prey for falconers is quite doubtful.

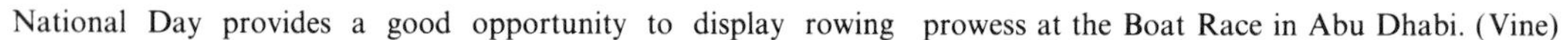

Preparing for traditional long boat races on the beach at Abu Dhabi with the modern skyline stretching into the distance. (Vine)

National Day provides a good opportunity to display rowing prowess at the Boat Race in Abu Dhabi. (Vine)

Oars are made ready with great care for the big race. (Vine)

The sleek wooden craft lies waiting for its complement of crew before the race begins. (Vine)

The long boat crew are poised and ready. (Vine)

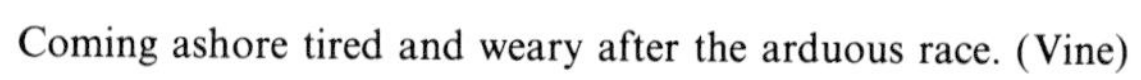

Coming ashore tired and weary after the arduous race. (Vine)

SOCIAL CUSTOMS

Despite the transformation brought about in the UAE by oil revenues, much has remained constant in the fabric of society. Of course life is vastly more comfortable for everybody, but attitudes, values, behaviour and customs forged under quite different circumstances and cemented by Islam, continue to be essential to both family and business life and to the local population's relationship with the newly created state. Islam is the rock, the foundation on which the state is built, its customs, dictates and practices are central to the fledgling federation, but tolerance and respect for other people's beliefs has also been a major characteristic of the sheikdoms in this area.

Politeness and courtesy to guests, whether family friends or business contacts is still a very noticeable feature of life in the UAE. Elaborate and extended greetings, liberally sprinkled with words of gratitude to God and often accompanied, between friends, by an embrace or a kiss on the cheek, are in stark contrast to the secular curt acknowledgments of the western world. Abundant hospitality, born of the harsh and lonely desert but entrenched by a religion which underlines its paramount importance, continues to be a vital aspect of life here. In the past, guests were welcomed to join in the traditional **mansaf** of whole lamb and spiced rice laid on trays on the floor of desert tent or urban house, eating with the right hand from communal dishes. Arabic coffee (**ghawah**), poured from distinctively-shaped coffee pots was always served at the end of the meal and, despite the gradual change from floor to table-eating with individual place settings, the aromatic and sugarless coffee is still a very important feature of Arab hospitality. Coffee, and indeed any light refreshment may be offered at any time in the shops or at the office: folk coffee-houses, in the old days, were the meeting and entertainment places in the Gulf complete with **gaduo**—the traditional smoking pot (or hubble bubble).

The **majilis** has also grown from hospitable practices of the desert; there was always one section of the bedouin camp where people congregated to talk and to share a special meal. Part of the tradition surrounding the **majilis** is that everyone is welcome. But great importance is also attached to family privacy, so as houses became more substantial, a special room in which to receive guests was deemed essential. This reception room known as the **majilis**, (often two—one for women and one for men) was kept for the celebration of formal occasions, or the entertainment of important guests. Traditionally open and spacious, with oriental carpets and cushions, the modern **majilis** usually has seating arranged around the walls. However the **majilis** is more than just a space or room for receiving guests, it is also something of a social institution mirroring the egalitarian nature of the older tribal society. The **majilis** of ruling sheikhs are splendidly and exotically furnished but are open to all from the poorest nomad to the richest merchant. Special sittings on certain days (especially the Eid) are arranged when visitors usually gather in an anteroom and move forward in a long queue to greet their host, to show their respect, make a complaint, or present a petition. Refreshments are served whilst guests sit around the room talking to their neighbours. As the **majilis** comes to an end, incense burners wafting scented smoke are brought around, filling the air, hair and clothes with a sweet fragrance, promoting a sense of relaxed well-being, and signalling the end of the majilis. Rosewater is also sprinkled on each guest's head and hands as they leave.

TRADITIONAL DRESS

Traditional costumes, one of the oldest art forms and an integral part of the folk culture of any society are usually dictated by a country's climatic and religious requirements, achieving a corresponding level of sophistication in material and elaboration as one climbs the social scale. The UAE corresponds to this pattern but it is unusual in that traditional dress is still the norm rather than relegated to the realms of folklore. Men traditionally wear an ankle-length, cool, loose-fitting and supremely comfortable garment, the **kandoura** or **dish-dash** complete with a high neck and long sleeves whilst a headdress, comprised of a skull-cap (**taqia** or **qahfa**) covered by a long cloth, usually white, (**gutra**) all secured by a wool rope (**al iqal** or **al ghizam**) wound round the crown, protects the head and neck from the blistering sun. The **bisht**, a sleeveless flowing black or beige cloak trimmed with gold, whose material depends on the social status of the wearer, is sometimes worn, especially for ceremonial occasions. The fact that this form of traditional dress is still used, with minor variation, throughout the Arabian peninsula is a sure tribute to its comfort and suitability for the difficult desert climate, even though this is now alleviated by extensive air-conditioning. But it also points to the pride people have in their particular Arab identity.

In addition to the clothes outlined above, bedouin men were usually attired with weaponry of one kind or another. The **khanjar**, a curving double-edged blade, six to eight inches long, with hilt of local horn overlaid with silver strips, was

A silver dagger, the **khanjar**, was once the formal wear for men of the region. (Kay)

once necessary for defensive purposes but has rapidly become a status symbol. The **khanjar's** curving wooden scabbard, is more extensively decorated, the upper part usually with engraved silver, the lower section consisting of strips of leather overlaid with silver and decorated with silver rings and wire, often in a geometric pattern and capped with a silver tip. Scabbards of a more recent manufacture employ gold for decoration. A single-edged tapering blade dagger with straight carved wood scabbard, silver overlaid at both ends is popular with the Shihuh of Ras Al Khaimah, as is the **yirz**, an axe combining a three-foot shaft with a four-inch steel head: the **saif**, a double-edged sword and the scimitar-like **qattara** are usually only seen in museums or in ceremonial dance. Silver and copper too was used to decorate containers for gun-powder and long-barrelled pistols. Bedouin men also carried more benign items such as beautifully decorated silver purses, pipes, toothpicks, ear-cleaning spoons and tweezers, all hanging from silver chains. Modern rifles and cartridge belts slung around the waist were eventually added to the customary dress of the Bedouin: like the **khanjar** these too were used for defensive purposes but are now mainly a status symbol.

Women dress according to their lifestyle and in accordance with Islamic ordinances. Like the male attire, traditional dress is still very popular. The original and versatile designs have hardly altered through the centuries, although there have been some fashion swings in the kinds of materials used. Bedouin women, for practical and monetary reasons, choose wool and cotton for their garments whereas the women of the town adorn themselves with silks, brocades, satins and chiffons. Women's clothing combines modesty and flamboyance, utility and elegance with a strong emphasis on intricate decoration. The **burqa,** a veil of coarse, black silk with a central stiffened rib resting on the nose allowing only the eyes to be clearly seen, is still worn in the street, particularly by older women. **Mashakhes** made from gold adorn the **burkha** and **al kaleeb** are sewn on both sides to fasten it up on the face. An all-enveloping black **abaya** is made from lightweight cloth embroidered with tapestried threads. The **kandoura,** a loose full-sleeved dress reaching to mid-calf, exquisitely embellished with **khawar** and **talla** on cuffs and collar, is usually of colourful material, quality and design varying with the economic status of the wearer. **Al serwal,** loose fitting trousers tight on the calves, worn under the **kandoura** are also beautifully decorated, this time with **'al badla' and 'swaiiyat um khudud'.** But the **thaub,** a full-length loose overdress of delicate chiffon, lavishly decorated, is surely the 'pièce de résistance'. Women make the most of their eyes and hands as these are often the only female flesh to be seen. Eyes are beautifully accentuated with kohl, whilst the palms of the hands and sometimes the soles of the feet are stained in intricate designs applied with henna.

Jewellery, like costume, is an ancient art form combining intrinsic art value and functional purpose. Not only was jewellery used by the women of the lower Gulf for adornment, but it had amuletic functions as well as providing financial security in the absence of banking facilities; many tribal women still carry their savings around necks, wrists or ankles. Silver was once the most valued metal often obtained from melted down Marie Therese dollars, renowned for a high and reliable silver content. Intricately designed necklets formed from beads and coins; elaborate forehead decorations of coins and chains; earrings of ornate circular loops or dangling shapes including inverted pyramids with embossed geometric designs; heavy bossed bracelets covering much of the

Fine necklace with silver Koran case. (Kay)

lower arm; elaborate hinged anklets, often with tinkling bells; rings for fingers, toes and even noses, sometimes inset with bone or horn and studded with stone, glass or coral; all adorned tribal women thoughout the ages. Many designs, common also to the jewellery of other areas, such as Oman, Baluchistan, India, Yemen, Saudi Arabia and East Africa, involve techniques used by ancient civilisations. These include chasing and engraving, piercing, filigree and granulation, necessitating the soldering of tiny silver balls to a base. Many fine examples of silver bedouin jewellery can still be found in markets and museums but gold jewellery, draped in tumultuous profusion in the gold souks of the Emirates, has since replaced silver in importance.

MUSIC, SONG AND DANCE

Oral tradition, dictated by the largely nomadic lifestyle of the Bedu is central to Arab cultural heritage. Creative inspiration found expression in folktales, proverbs, parables, poetry and song often accompanied by music and dance. Saad Abdullah Sowayan in his beautifully written book on the expressive lyrical oral poetry, composed in the

Glittering gold jewellery of intricate traditional design on sale in the Gold Souks of the Emirates. (Vine)

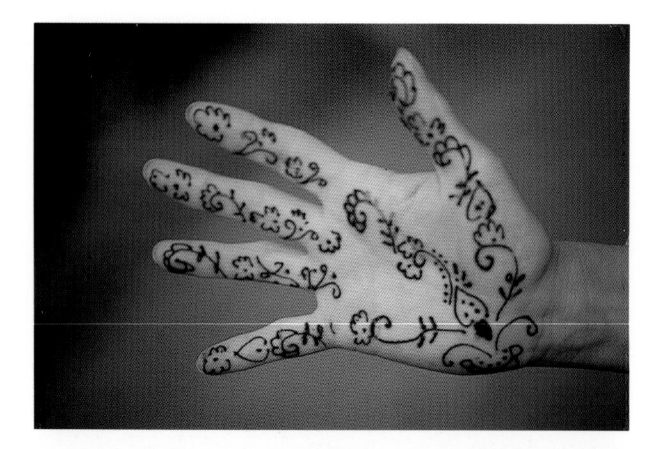

Henna is stained on hands and feet for weddings and other festivals. Traditionally simple geometric designs have given place to ornate flower patterns of Indian influence. (Kay)

vernacular, we now know as Nabati poetry explains how this form of creative expression was to be found in all walks of life.

"*In premodern Arabia there was considerable reliance on the well-developed and highly stylised idiom of Nabati poetry as a means of communication, especially on solemn or formal occasions. Tribal chiefs and town amirs as well as relatives and friends communicated with one another in poems. Tribal territories, grazing areas, water holes, desert roads and stations; grievances, threats, battles, and other events, large and small - all were recorded and described in poems.*" Arabic singing was possibly derived from the **hudaa** - the verse sung by a performer to entertain and encourage desert travellers on long caravan journeys. But bedouin singing is neither simple nor monotonous as the uninitiated might be led to believe. The rich and varied lifestyle, enjoyed by these desert inhabitants, has produced a wide range of singing styles, some lending themselves to musical accompaniment through exposure to other cultural influences.

Song, music and dance was not limited to casual entertainment or even, as in Nabati poetry, to an attempt to come to grips with the harsh realities of life: the singing of rhythmical chants provided a method of easing the burden of communal work as exemplified by the work songs of pearl divers in the Gulf. Singing was also the main source of comfort for the men engaged in the pearl fishery, helping them to bear the rigours of life on board pearling vessels, compounded by long and painful separation from their families. There was a specific singing form attached to each particular task: hauling the anchor, manoeuvering the oars, extending the jib sail, raising the mainsail, and the actual pearl diving. The **nahham** was the the leading performer and coordinator of all the pearling songs, but his role was much more than that of mere virtuoso, he was the one who comforted, consoled and entertained the crew, attempting to lighten both their hearts and the arduous tasks ahead of them through the ecstasy of rhythym. Crew members repeated all the refrains whilst the **tabl** (a longitudinal drum with two skins), the **tas** (a tin bowl) and hand-clapping were used to accentuate the long, contemplative rhythmic cycles of these unique work songs.

In contrast, the short rhythmic songs belong to the Bedu - two major styles here are the lyrical **khammari (la'buni)** and **samri** and the proud and war-like **ardah.** Music and and dance accompanying these songs also had an important ritualistic and social function as exemplified by the male dance **Ayyalah al Ardha** and women's song and dance performances, usually performed at weddings. The **Ayyalah al-Ardha,** a ceremonial war dance, is still performed in the UAE as well as in other parts of the Gulf, although under a different title. The **Ayyalah** dance simulates a battle scene with 2-4 rows of male dancers wielding sticks as swords and moving forwards and backwards, alternately signifying victory and defeat. Drums and percussions provide the rhythmic beat whilst a group of female performers - the **na'ashat** - cheer the other participants.

The rhythm and text of some of the collective dances betray strong African influence communicated by immigrant populations and sea-trading contacts: the '**lewah**', for instance, may well have originated in Nubia in the Sudan. Performed to the accompaniment of drums and a flute-like instrument - the **sernay** - by groups of males and females, some original Swahili vocabulary still persists in the text of the songs. The actual form the dance will take depends on whether the **lewah** is being performed for general public entertainment or on special occasions.

Tambourines and drums which accompany the dance are heated before a fire to tauten the skin. (Kay)

CONSTRUCTION AND DESIGN

The bedouin tent is familiar to most people. A useful and adaptable structure, it was woven from goat hair and sheep wool, not by professional weavers but by the women of the family as required. But the airy tent was not the only mobile structure used for housing in the Gulf. **Barasti** houses made of palm fronds, mangrove poles and cord, sometimes with foundations of stone, could also be occupied on a temporary basis for the date harvest, or the fishing season, and moved as required. In some instances, these cool houses were developed into more sophisticated establishments, taking on some of the features of permanent homes, such as windtowers made from wood and canvas. Recently **barasti** construction has been given a new lease of life by the importation of 'prefabricated' sections of matting for the construction of side-flaps which can be raised or lowered as required to achieve maximum ventilation.

Traditional housing, no more than traditional costume, is very much the product of social custom and climate, although, of course, the availability of material had an impact on construction and design. Fossilised coral, cut in blocks, bonded with **sarooj,** a blend of Iranian red clay and manure, or a lime mixture derived from sea shells, and plastered with chalk and water paste, was used extensively in coastal regions. These materials have very low thermal conductivity and were therefore ideally suited to the hot and humid coastal environment. Mud brick and stone featured extensively in construction inland. Arab hospitality dictated the inclusion of large open spaces in the design of local houses but religious requirements demanded privacy for the women of

Traditional folk-dance, performed at weddings. (Kay)

An unusual round wind-tower gracing the skyline of Sharjah's old souk area has been ear-marked for restoration work. (Vine).

Traditional door and padlock on an old house in Sharjah. (Vine).

the family. These conflicting demands were met by the designation of two separate areas for men and women opening on a central common courtyard: this internal court, in more sophisticated houses overlooked by elaborately screened balconies, also facilitated the circulation of cool air. Elaborate sculpted plaster work was often used as a decorative device but wood ornamentation is thought to be an even older art form. Both wooden and plasterwork screens give a certain amount of protection and privacy but also diffuse and deflect the harsh sunlight so that a pleasing pattern of light and shade is achieved. Islam forbids the imitation of any figurative or life-like forms, as a result much artistic expression was directed into ornamentation depicting orthodox geometric patterns, floral design, and calligraphy. Wood was extremely scarce in the Gulf region, therefore it was basically the privileged few who could afford imported woods for carving. The cheaper 'Sandy' teak, as opposed to 'Mountain' teak used in the dhow-building yards, was favoured for decorative screens, windows and doors. In the grander establishments, upper windows were often fronted by elaborately carved bays and protected from the harsh sun and prying eyes by carved wooden louvres. But wood was both scarce and expensive so that most furniture, such as four-poster beds, kitchen cupboards, and large chests were imported. Decorated wooden objects were much cherished items, often becoming valued family heirlooms.

Wind-towers **(badgeer),** introduced by Persian immigrants in the nineteenth century, were the really unique architectural feature of Gulf houses. In Dubai, especially the Bastakia district, these tall angular, structures, designed to increase air movement in the rooms below, are still very much in evidence rising in splendour from the roofs of old merchant houses. But large houses elsewhere (as well as forts) also took advantage of their unique cooling abilities. Tomkinson eloquently describes the the workings of these fuel-free 'air-conditioners'.... "*every face of the four-square tower is hollowed, usually into a concave V-shape. In Dubai many wind-towers are like medieval louvres, each facet a series of recesses fronted by a squat colonnade. The wind, from whichever quarter hits one of the walls and is deflected down the hollow shaft to the rooms below.*" The vents of the wind-tower can be shut when cool air is not required. Although much of the extensive new building taking place in the UAE follows a bold, new, high-rise format dictated by modern building techniques and up-to-date cooling technology, some

Opposite: Coral blocks, shell rubble and lime plaster were convenient materials used in many old buildings in the UAE. (Vine)

new private villas and public buildings, such as the enclosed souk at Khorfakkan, have opted for a more ornate traditional design complete with windtowers.

Many examples of simple but splendid forts, mentioned already in the historical section, add to the variety of indigenous buildings in the Emirates. Most are built of mud-brick, quadrilateral in plan, with square or round towers situated at each corner and an imposing entrance dominating one side. Heavy wooden doors studded with large iron spikes and complicated locking mechanisms usually secure these openings: sometimes a verse from the Holy Quran is inscribed into a panel above the door. Ras Al Khaimah's forts differ in so much as stone from the many local quarries is utilised in their construction. Some of these old defensive structures have been sensitively renovated with traditional materials and are being used as museums and documentation centres.

Mosques, like houses, were traditionally relatively simple structures capped by short and unornamented minarets. However, the enormous number of new mosques (at least two thousand have been built since independence as concrete evidence of the universal and deep commitment to the Islamic faith) are much more heavily ornamented structures topped by graceful, slender, minarets. These new mosques range in style and design from tiny exquisite structures such as the Indian-influenced white mosque decorated with delicate lacy plasterwork, which is situated in the centre of Sharjah, to the vast King Faisal Mosque, accommodating 5,000 worshippers and incorporating an Islamic centre, also in the centre of Sharjah. In between are medieval stone architectural masterpieces and stark simple modern designs.

It is obvious that, although life in the UAE has achieved a high level of comfort and sophistication, tradition still holds a firm place in the lives of its people, providing a sense of security and continuity amidst the hectic bustle of modern life.

Entrance to Dubai's Museum, housed inside Al Fahidi Fort. (Vine).

Door knocker on door at Dubai Museum. (Vine).

ART AND ARTISTS*

The art movement in the United Arab Emirates is similar in development to that of its counterparts in other Gulf states, as far as artistic styles, ideas or even affiliations to various art schools are concerned.

The social history of the Emirates has had a major influence on art development, since most of its population, until quite recently, has consisted of tent-dwelling nomadic Bedouins whose rugged lifestyle involved a perpetual search of the essentials for their survival. This led to a preeminence of spoken or literal arts accompanied by rather slow development of fine or plastic arts. Only in very recent years did many people settle in towns, forming an urban society. Important exceptions to this general observation are the coastal regions such as Dubai and Sharjah and it is interesting to note that these still lead the national art movement.

Recording the country's rich cultural heritage in its various forms, including the details of peoples daily lives, still provides a major inspirational source for the UAE artist. These subjects, so closely connected with the recent past, are understood and deeply appreciated by today's society. To some extent this has placed a limit upon the development of art, with those artists who seek a wider source of subject matter likely to experience difficulties with marketing their work. One result of this has been that many artists have tended to experiment with media rather than subjects.

Both the Ministry of Education and the Ministry of Information and Culture have played a significant part in nurturing the nation's art movement. The former provided scholarships enabling local artists such as Mohammed Youssif, Hamed Al Suweidi, Obaid Suroor and Mohamed Mendi to study in Cairo whilst Ibrahim Mustapha and Salim Johar were sent to Baghdad. The latter provides assistance and encouragement for artists to mount exhibitions throughout the year. Two prominent names which spring to mind in this regard are Issam Al Sheradi and Abdul Karim Sukar, who influenced the development of art through their positions as supervisors of the exhibitions department in the Ministry of Information and Culture. Their efforts resulted in many art exhibitions, in some of which they themselves participated. A great deal of interest in and support for the UAE art movement has also derived from the presence of non- UAE artists such as Saad Al Moussawi; Mounira Toukan; Ihsan Al Khatib and Mohamed Al Shakfa together with others.

In 1980 the UAE Association for Illustrative Art was established; initially under the presidency of Mohamed Youssif, followed by Hamed Al Suweidi, and, at the time of writing, headed by Abdul Rahmin Salim. In the same year the new association staged its first major exhibition featuring artists such as Obaid Suroor, Ibrahim Mustapha, Mohamed Youssif, Hamed Al Suweidi, Hassan Al Sharif, Ahmed Al Ansari, Abdul Qadir Idris and many other Arab artists residing in the UAE. Since its inception, the Association has provided a focus for the activities of national artists and has played a crucial role in development of the national art movement. Communications with other Arab art groups have been fostered by attendance at conferences and meetings throughout the Arab world, creating opportunities for interaction with other artists and promoting a two way flow of ideas, knowledge and experience.

In 1985 the First UAE National Art Exhibition was held, coinciding with the opening of an art department at the Cultural Foundation in Abu Dhabi. The event is now established as an annual exhibition open to all amateur and professional artists. In their efforts to further encourage art development, the Cultural Foundation followed-up on this major exhibition by organising annual art exhibitions for special interest groups leading to events such as the annual UAE Youth Exhibition and the UAE Women's Exhibition launched

**This introduction has been written by Reem El-Mutwalli*

Abdul Rahim Salem

in 1985 together with the Al Rabi'a Photography Exhibition, first held in 1986. These activities have encouraged individual artists to hold personal exhibitions at the Centre, further stimulating a local interest in the arts.

The Abu Dhabi Cultural Foundation has drawn upon its experience in the region's art movement to mount its own study of the development and progress of the arts leading to comprehensive documentation of UAE artists and their work. In late 1985 a new education programme was established with the aim of enhancing awareness and appreciation of art in the UAE. This programme continues to operate, teaching talented school children and adults the basics of fine arts by special courses involving lectures, practical studio work, films and seminars.

While the art movement is still young, foundations have been well laid for it to maintain its current momentum. In this it will continue to derive strength and direction from the different artists and organisations involved in the process; united in their mutual desire to achieve a single goal: a healthy and vigorous art community in the United Arab Emirates.

Abdul Rahim Salem

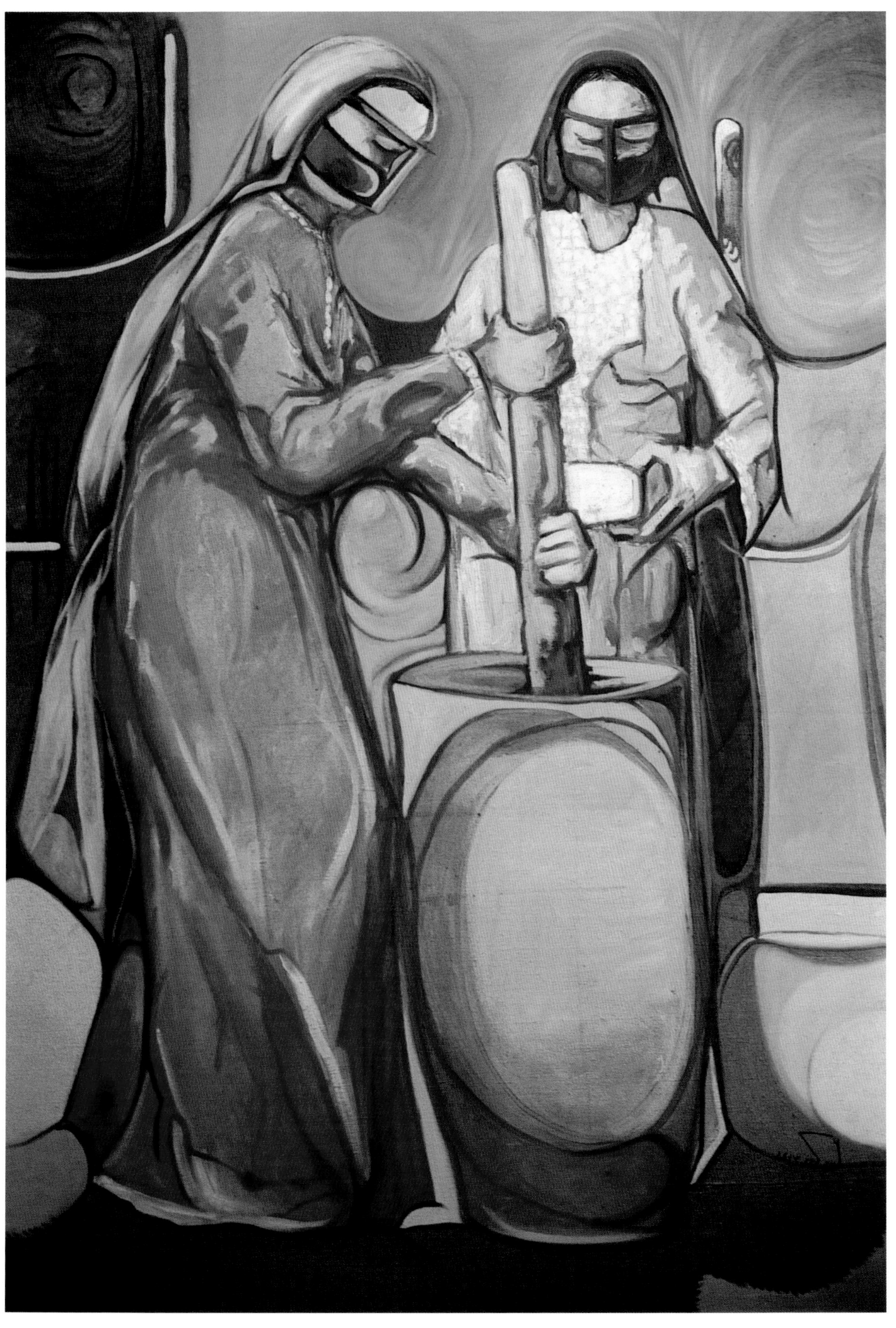

Obaid Surour

Obaid Surour

Mohamed Yousef

Mohamed Mandi

Mohamed Al Qasab

Hassan Sharif

Hassan Sharif

Mona Al Khaja

Nejaht Hassan Makki

Khouloud Salih

Khouloud Salih

Mahmoud Al Ramahi

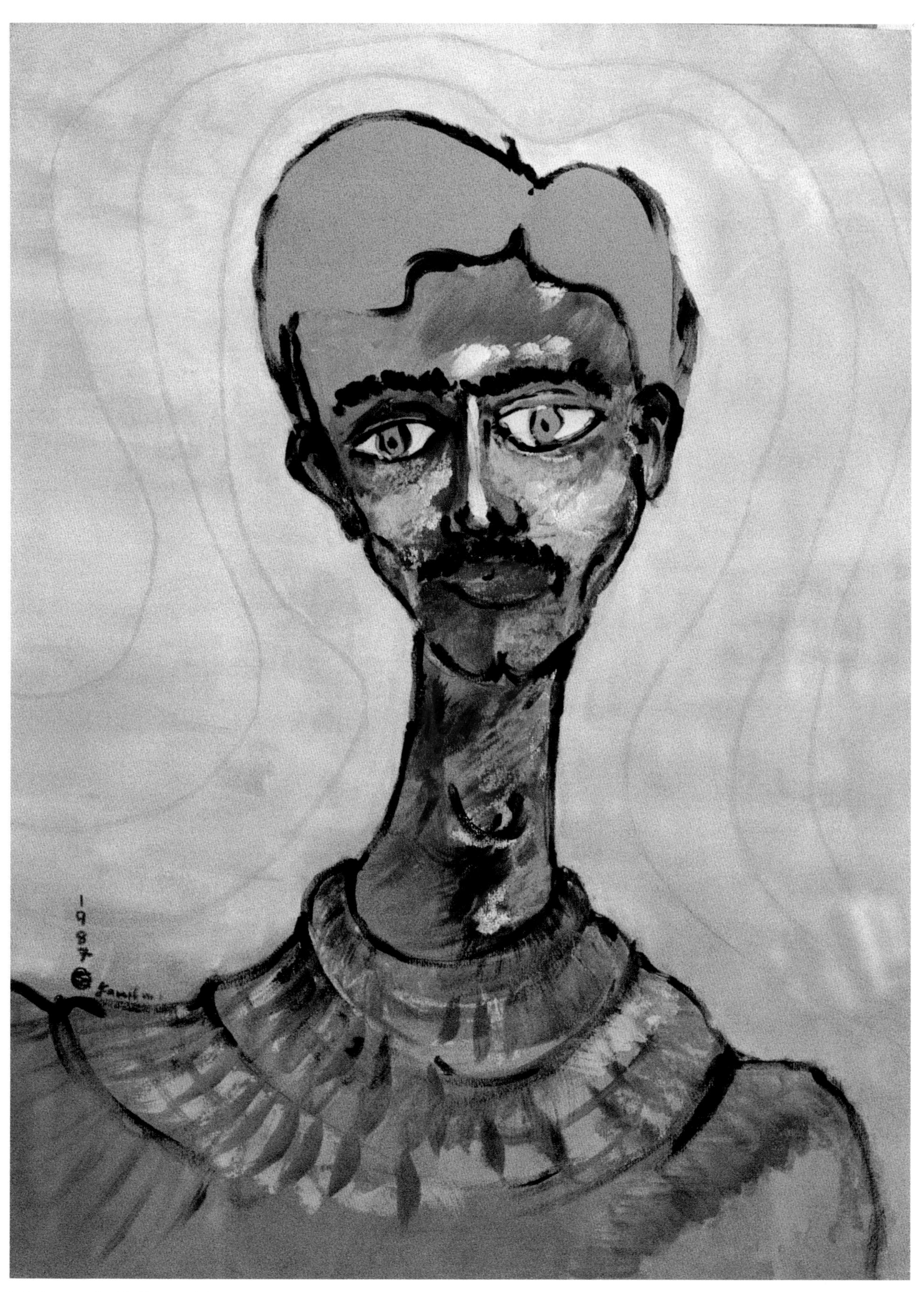

Mahmoud Al Ramahi

Ibrahim Al Sharhan

Hisham Al Mathloum

Mohamed Khadim

Nasser Abdullah

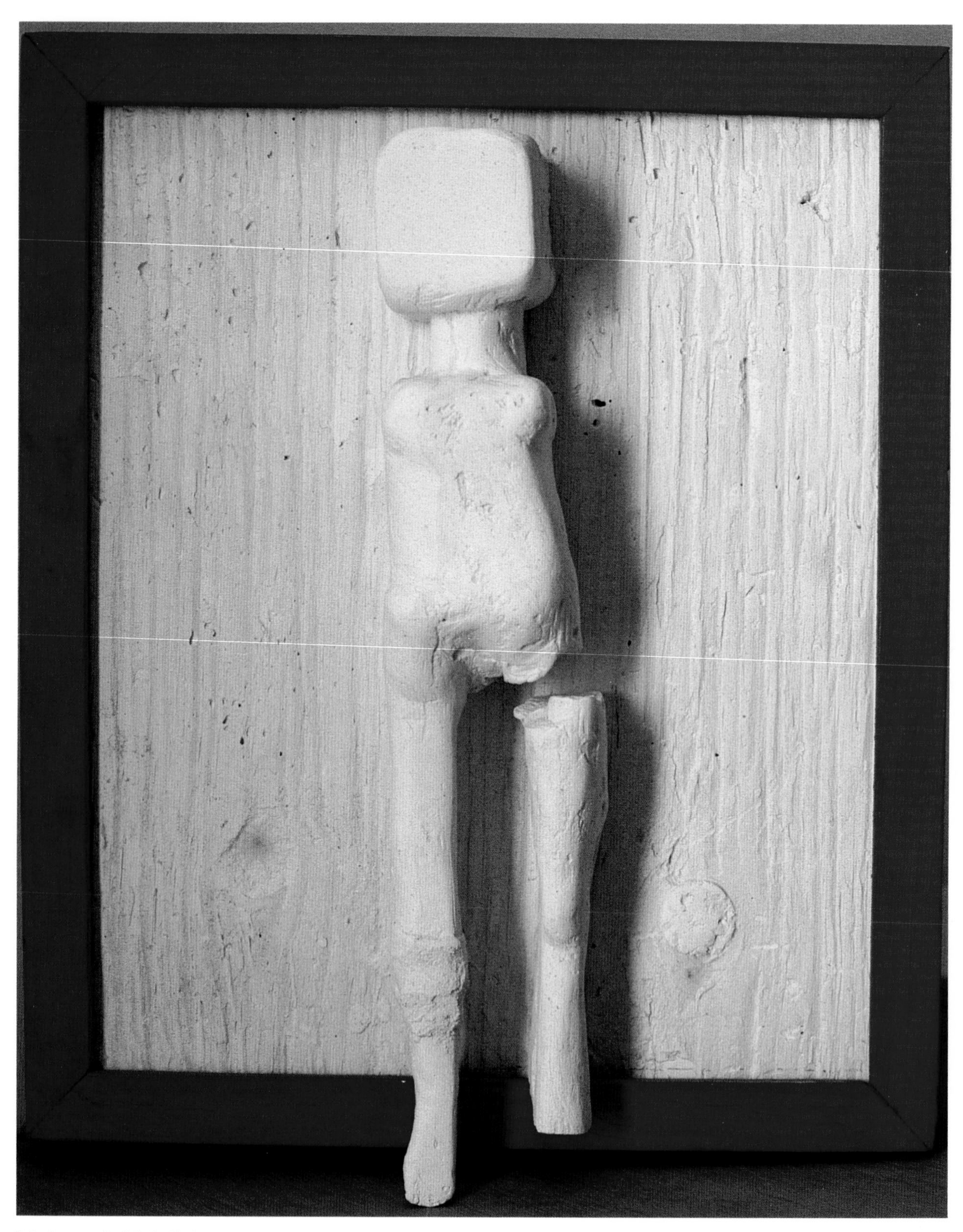

Mohamed Abdullah

MODERN EMIRATES

The design of Emirates Golf House, opened in 1988, is based upon the form of traditional Bedouin tents. (Vine).

Few countries can match the astonishing progress made by the United Arab Emirates through the last two decades. Today the UAE, although still in its teens as a unified economic and political entity, is the business hub of the Middle East, home to scores of multinational trade and banking houses, as well as the world's largest man-made port. The country has risen to its present status at a bewildering pace since its formation in 1971 from seven independent emirates–Abu Dhabi, Dubai, Sharjah, Ajman, Umm Al Quwain, Ras Al Khaimah and Fujairah. The oil

Road constructors in the UAE were not allowed to forget the country's oldest means of transport, the camel. (Vine)

Imposing main entrance of Sharjah's recently completed new corniche souk. (Vine).

boom has brought enormous benefit to the UAE, but petroleum and gas exports are by no means the sole factors behind the country's advancement. The rush of oil was accompanied by a flurry of construction. Industrial plants sprang up around the country: one producing hundreds of thousands of tons of aluminium a year also delivers millions of gallons of desalinated water every day to the people of the UAE, as a by-product. High technology arrived in various forms, and the biggest dry docks in the world were built at Dubai to service ships, using the most modern methods available. At the same time, the UAE has gone through monumental changes in healthcare, education and agriculture, with hospitals and clinics, schools and universities sprouting around the country, like the wheat now growing across previously barren desert plains. Water, liquid gold in desert regions and traditionally in short supply, is now plentiful thanks to numerous desalination plants and the most modern irrigation techniques. Similarly, electricity has reached all corners of the Emirates, providing the power to maintain progress.

The UAE and its people have taken all these changes in their stride, ever mindful of the need to move with the times, but equally vigilant at

Goods arrive in the Emirates by land, sea and air and are sold or trans-shipped here to serve local and foreign markets. One of the UAE's most atmospheric harbour scenes is along the creek road at Deira where beautiful wooden dhows still crowd the wharf, advertising passage to other Arabian ports, or loading and offloading their cargoes. (Vine)

Classic architecture is a feature of many new buildings in the UAE. Here the use of lanterns cleverly enhances the facade, emphasising the traditional roots of an Arabian market. (Vine).

ensuring their past is not forgotten. Their centuries old culture has been guarded as eagerly as any priceless heritage. Although the architects of the space-age have undoubtedly changed the face of their homeland, their designs reflect the restraining hand of tradition. In fact, some of the most splendid and classically-shaped buildings now standing alongside the modern streets and highways of the UAE were built in the last few years. There are many fine examples of how old and new have merged happily, none better than the magnificent new souk at Sharjah. A maze of clumsy stalls and mud-brick shops has been replaced by a purpose-built souk, retaining the most admired qualities of Islamic architecture, while still reflecting all the advantages of 20th century practicality. Dozens upon dozens of shops are contained inside its walls of rich mosaic and towering arches, offering a bountiful collection of gold and silver, jewellery and antiques, cloth and carpets. There are also digital watches, colour televisions and the latest hi-fi's–some of the souk's best bargains come in stereo!

Mosque in dramatic setting at Sha'am, Ras Al Khaimah. (Vine)

Mosques of the UAE are symbols of the people's fervent adherence to a religious code that guides them through life. Large or small, old or new, they are a constant reminder of the presence of Islam. They too reflect how the past and present live comfortably together in the UAE. While the religious habits of the people have gone unchanged over the years, many of the beautiful new mosques which worshippers enter today, although retaining all their classical features, have a fresh, glowing look about them. Modern amplifiers help to sound the call of Allah-u-Akbar from the city minarettes, sending it echoing across the land, past scores of forts and watchtowers and peaceful fishing villages where the day's catch is all-important, to the base of the rugged Hajar mountains, stretching from the Gulf coast to the shores of the Indian Ocean.

One of the best aspects of modern UAE is that, despite its impressive achievements, its people have not abandoned their traditional Arab values. In a world where the influences of urbanisation are eroding family-life, spiritual and social traditions, it is extremely heartening to discover that these aspects are held in high esteem in the Emirates.

Given the degree to which the past is cherished, it is all the more surprising how well the future has been planned. Whilst it is true that oil

The Islamic faith continues to play a vital role in the UAE, providing spiritual guidance to its people. Some of the country's finest local architecture is to be found in its mosques, as in this example from Al Ain. (Vine)

The city of Abu Dhabi has been transformed from a dusty, sandy town to a modern city adorned by attractive public gardens and architecturally innovative buildings. (Vine)

has provided much of the finance for the economic miracle of UAE's development, it must also be stated that full credit is due to the government for prudent and well-planned use of the available resources.

In his excellent account of the earliest archaeological investigations of the region, 'Looking for Dilmun', Geoffrey Bibby writes as follows of his first visit to Abu Dhabi in 1958. "*I shall always be glad that I saw Abu Dhabi before the oil came in three years later. For as Abu Dhabi was then, so must all the towns of the Gulf have been before the great oil adventure started. There had been no passport or customs officials at the airport. There was in fact no air service; the strip had been built for the oil company and the only planes to use it were those chartered by the oil company. And there was no road from the airstrip to the town. At the edge of the salt-flat the sand began, deep, white and floury. The Land-Rovers, on low pressure tyres, ground downward through the low register of gears, ploughing with their four-wheel drive hub-deep through the drift-sand. Ahead, a single line of palm-trees stood incongruously in the sand, with the bulk of the whitewashed fort to the left and with the cluster of barastis beyond. We slid between the trees and among the huts, with rangy hens and lean goats scattering before us, and donkeys browsing incuriously on scraps of paper in the shadow of barasti fences. Winding among the huts, the furrows in the sand which alone marked the road led out to the shore between two white cement buildings, the po-*

The Intercontinental Hotel chain has hotels in Abu Dhabi, Al Ain and Dubai and in each the chain's renowned standards of comfort and service are rigorously maintained. (Vine)

lice headquarters and the office of the oil company. This was the centre of the town....."

Each emirate has developed its own particular character, based upon its natural resources and the priorities of individual rulers. Abu Dhabi, ruled by His Highness, Sheikh Zayed bin Sultan al Nahyan, President of the UAE, is the largest of the seven, with a land area of approximately 67,340 sq. kms. First among the UAE member states to export oil as recently as 1962, it possesses the lion's share of oil and gas reserves, most of which are situated offshore, in the shallow waters of the Gulf, serviced from the industrialised Das island and from main offices in Abu Dhabi. Other islands within the emirate include Sa'adiyat, east of the capital, where an agricultural research station is situated, and Umm an Nar, once an ancient dispersal point for valuable copper resources, now the location of a major oil refinery.

The main city of Abu Dhabi, supporting a population of approximately 400,000 is situated on the coast, like most of the major settlements in the Emirates. Provisional capital of the United Arab Emirates, it is home for many business headquarters together with government departments connected both with Abu Dhabi itself, and with the federal government of the UAE The Abu Dhabi National Oil Company also has its headquarters here. Whilst a massive building programme has taken place to provide offices for government administration and private business, and a modern road network has been established, the city has avoided becoming a concrete jungle. Instead, the municipality has placed great emphasis upon beautification, achieving remarkable results in this area, creating verdant public gardens, flower and shrub-lined main roads, and many attractive fountains or street sculptures. The green-belt around the city now extends from the unique corniche to Musaffah and is supported by a number of model nurseries. Luxuriant gardens surrounding many magnificent private residences and mosques compliment the efforts of the public authority to create a green and pleasant city.

Abu Dhabi, like the other emirates, has made major strides in the field of health and education and the provision of adequate housing, water and electricity to all its citizens. It has also developed numerous sophisticated leisure facilities, ranging from the Abu Dhabi Cultural Foundation to many impressive sports complexes, crowned by the huge Sports City. In fact most of the major sports are played here, from soccer, cricket, golf, and tennis to windsurfing, sailing and diving in the warm waters of the Gulf.

Shopping is a joy in Abu Dhabi whether in large

In Abu Dhabi's old Souk. (Vine)

The Intercontinental Hotel, Abu Dhabi, like many modern hotels in the UAE, offers clients the ultimate standards of comfort and relaxation. (Vine)

A large water fountain on Abu Dhabi corniche resembles a volcano, especially when illuminated. This has become a popular meeting place for residents on their evening stroll. (Vine)

Zayed Sports City is one of the most modern sporting structures in Arabia, including a mammoth stadium and first class football pitch together with numerous other facilities. (Vine)

well-appointed stores, stocked with luxury goods or the more traditional souks, redolent with the atmosphere of the Middle East and full of cascading gold jewellery, cameras, watches and exotic carpets - all at bargain prices. An elegantly constructed corniche provides residents with the opportunity to escape from the bustle of the down-town commercial and shopping centre and to enjoy the fresh sea breeze while observing maritime activities along its shore-line. Wind-surfers and sea-scooters wend their way between more traditional craft and the maritime heritage of Abu Dhabi is especially well preserved in the dhow building yards of Batin close to the prestigious Intercontinental Hotel. Abu Dhabi has its fair share of luxury hotels, complete with extensive leisure facilities, sophisticated, modern conference suites and excellent restaurants, featuring local and international cuisine. A host of international show-business stars playing to capacity crowds adds to the cosmopolitan night-life of these hotels.

Al Ain situated amongst the large Al Ain-Buraimi oasis, birthplace of His Highness, Sheikh Zayed, is the second city of Abu Dhabi, supporting a population of approximately 150,000. The National University located here is seen as the crowning glory of a rapidly advancing educational system. The considerable influx of people, generated by the presence of the University has brought benefits for the municipality of Al-Ain. Like Abu Dhabi, Al Ain has been transformed by horticultural activities creating a green and beautiful city containing at least thirty-six well kept public gardens. It is also the site of considerable agricultural activity using modern methods to capitalise on the skill and knowledge of the past. The new museum at Al Ain houses numerous interesting finds from extensive archaeological excavations in the rich hinterland including the oldest monumental sites in the Emirates. A well-designed Zoo complete with Aquarium, and a modernistic "Fun City" standing in stark contrast to the traditional bustle of the Camel Market, all add to the attractions of 'Al Ain.

A water-scooter zips across the water alongside Abu Dhabi's corniche. (Vine)

The fishing boat area of Abu Dhabi's shoreline is crowded with modern fishing vessels. (Vine)

Bordered on its western extremities by the warm clear waters of the Arabian Gulf, and encompassing stretches of still pristine desert, Abu Dhabi emirate is an exceedingly attractive place to live or visit.

Over the years Dubai has unwittingly collected a handful of credits, all claiming to encapsulate the true flavour of a business centre, port city and keeper of Arabic traditions rolled into one. Among the favourites are "Pearl of the Gulf", "Gem of the Arabian deserts", which in reality reveal little about the serious nature of a city bustling with activity. Dubai's stature as the commercial kernal of the region is confirmed by the presence of the towering International Trade Centre which can be seen for miles around the city, standing out like a beacon as if to symbolise the emirate's rapid rise in the business world.

Part of the reason for Dubai's success story lies in the far-sightedness of its ruler, H.H. Sheikh Rashid bin Saeed Al Maktoum, who consulted the business community during preparation of his

Almost every city in the Emirates sports a clock-tower as a central feature of the town. This one is in Al Ain, second city of the Emirate of Abu Dhabi. (Vine)

Dubai's Trade Centre dwarfs all other high-rise offices in Dubai and neighbouring Deira, the commercial heart of the United Arab Emirates. (Vine)

grand plan for a thriving metropolis on the shores of the Arabian Gulf. Today the Creek, the tidal inlet responsible for Dubai's birth, is fittingly the city's commercial centre, lined by office blocks, banks and other trading houses, and within hearing distance of the dealings taking place at the souk, the traditional market place. To attract business from around the world, Dubai set out to create a life-style for expatriates which would not only be acceptable to them, but would actually be regarded as highly desirable.

Miles of golden beaches, lapped by the rich blue waters of the Arabian Gulf, provide a natural asset of which Dubai has taken full advantage. With the arrival of five-star hotel accommoodation came the squash and tennis courts, swimming pools, saunas and jacuzzis–all of which are an established part of life in Dubai. Also, scattered about the city, are a cluster of sports complexes and clubs offering variety in leisure to a community that works hard and values the importance of leisure-time.

Attention to detail has been an important element in the development of Dubai, where handsome buildings stand rigidly to attention alongside wide luxuriantly planted avenues decorated by imaginative fountains. In Dubai's central business and shopping area, modern boutiques nestle in the shade generously provided by offices of high finance. Thirty minutes away by car stands perhaps the most vivid testimony to the city's indomitable will to succeed. The largest man-made port in the world dresses a wide body of coastline fronting the village of Jebel Ali, currently enticing a flow of global business. The creation of the Jebel Ali Free Trade Zone has attracted a stream of companies, all eager to take advantage of the concessions now readily available. Indeed, Dubai's mega-ports at Jebel Ali and Port Rashid underline the vital role the sea has played in Dubai's history and development. The emirate, taking in seventy-two kilometres of Gulf coastline, has its capital adjacent to Dubai creek, upon which stands the ancient city of Dubai and the commercial centre of Deira. With a total area of 3,885 sq. kilometres, Dubai occupies approximately five percent of the UAE's land area, a figure which belies the emirate's important status as the commercial and trading heart of the country—sixty percent of the UAE's imports come through Dubai.

On the southern shores of Dubai creek are the offices of the Ruler, H.H. Sheikh Mohammed Bin Rashid Al Maktoum, who is also Vice President

From the main Dubai–Abu Dhabi road Emirates Golf Club, near Jebel Ali, appears to drivers like a futuristic Bedouin settlement. (P. Vine).

UAE's beach resorts such as Chicago Beach Hotel south of Dubai city, offer residents and visitors an opportunity to cool off in the swimming pool, the sea, or under a refreshing shower! (P. Vine).

of the UAE. Administrative responsibilities are, however shared by Sheikh Rashid's four sons, Crown Prince Sheikh Maktoum (Deputy Federal Prime Minister), Sheikh Hamdam (Federal Minister of Finance and Industry); Sheikh Mohammed (Federal MInister of Defence) and Sheikh Ahmed, Commander of the Central Military Command of the UAE Armed Forces. Also situated on the southern shores, are most company headquarters and infrastructural facilities, including banks, customs, broadcasting and postal headquarters; all dwarfed by the huge sky-scraper of Dubai's thirty-nine storey International Trade Centre, the tallest building in the Gulf. The sister connurbation of Deira on the northern bank of the creek, is the main market centre and has the distinctive feature of numerous large trading dhows tied alongside the creek road, eloquently underlining Dubai's traditional role as a centre for trade and commerce. There are many bargains to be found in Deira's souk, a labyrinthine maze of snaking alleyways overlooked by windtowers, lined by beautifully carved wooden doors and filled with the pungent aroma of exotic spices and the haggling hum of

Hatta Fort Hotel is a favourite summer resort for many UAE residents where they enjoy cooler weather and stunning mountain scenery. (Vine).

bargain hunters. Both fish and fruit and vegetable souks are especially colourful and atmospheric as the early morning light slants over their shining produce. Trade in gold and pearls, particularly between Dubai and the enormous Indian market, was the traditional commercial backbone of Dubai. Today the gold souk in Deira continues to benefit from the same eastern appetite for this precious metal. The malleable, shining, material is beaten and cleverly fashioned by local craftsmen into elaborate traditional shapes but modern Italian-made jewellery is also readily available. Value for money is the hallmark too, of the less traditional shopping malls and modern stores. Whether one decides to shop in the old or the new, or both, glistening gold in startling profusion, tumbling colourful silks, elaborate brocades, the latest in cameras, watches, video and stereo equipment, antiques, souvenirs, delicious Arabic pastries and an immense variety of international foods will tantalise the prospective buyer.

Dubai is the second of the UAE's oil and gas producers. Like the other emirates it, too, has felt the effects of the dramatic fall in the price of oil since the beginning of 1986. But the emirate's rich hydrocarbon resources have helped to fuel a thriving local economy and diversified industrial development. DUBAL, a heavy industry project with both government and private shareholding produces high-grade aluminium from Western Australia bauxite utilising the abundant supply of cheap energy to fuel the process in one of the most energy efficient aluminium smelters in the world. As mentioned above, Dubai also boasts one of the largest dry-docks in the world. In addition to these two major projects, numerous private sector industries exist here, from cable manufacturers and steel milling to various plastic fabricators and a major cement producer.

The Jebel Ali Free Trade Zone referred to above is a tribute to the foresight of His Highness Sheikh Rashid, who had the vision and courage to give the go-ahead to the World's largest man-made port, comprising sixty seven berths along 15 kilometres of quays equipped with the most modern handling equipment. Companies relocating in Jebel Ali benefit also from a complete package of incentives including total ownership, extensive tax-free relief and a steady supply of free energy. The success of this project to date and the economic development it has fostered in the emirate, build on the timeless role free trade has played in bringing prosperity to Dubai.

Despite the emphasis on industry and trade, the building of numerous modern well-designed office buildings, shopping malls, exhibition centres and an extensive housing programme, an acute environmental awareness has succeeded in making Dubai green and beautiful. Flower-filled parks, tree-lined avenues and attractive recreation areas have ensured that Dubai is always a pleasant place to be. In line with a renewed emphasis on traditional roots and values, several old buildings are being lovingly renovated. In late 1986 the rebuilding of Sheikh Saeed's house, home of the former ruler and father of His Highness Sheikh Rashid was finished, restoring the lovely old coral stone building complete with windtowers and delightful decorative details, such as carved woodwork and pierced plaster screens, to its former glory. The impressive Dubai Museum also provides a link with a more ancient past. Amongst other interesting objects, it exhibits rich finds from the extensive cemetery and habitation mounds of the 2nd and 1st millenia BC. excavated at Al Qasais near Dubai.

Leisure facilities in Dubai include a superbly designed eighteen hole golf course (the first grass championship course in the Gulf), four 20,000 seater soccer stadiums, six sports complexes, two ice-skating rinks, camel and horse-racing tracks together with a go-cart circuit, a zoological park, and a mountain retreat at the Emirate's small, isolated enclave of Hatta. Dubai is also host to the Dubai International Car Rally, part of the Middle East Championship, and the Emirate's Dubai Powerboat Race, both among the richest in their class worldwide. At the time of writing Dubai is building an international sports complex

Al Fahidi Fort, almost two hundred years old, underwent a second major restoration effort in 1987 and 1988. The Museum within its coral-block walls was originally opened in 1971 and houses an interesting collection of artefacts from the region's past. (Vine).

holding a 22,000 seater cricket ground and a 9,500 capacity hockey stadium. The traditionally strong local interest in horses has blossomed into Dubai hosting the largest international horse show in the region, known as the "Hickstead of the Middle East"!

Numerous luxuriously appointed hotels, many fronting on private sandy beaches, offering a wide range of water sports, international restaurants and other attractions, coupled with technologically superior conference and exhibition centres make Dubai a particularly good place to visit for business or leisure. Dubai, like Abu Dhabi, has a thriving hotel-based night-life. Visiting entertainers range from the New York Metropolitan Opera, ballet, string quartets and chamber orchestras to world famous rock and comedy stars.

Dubai is blessed with a warm, sunny winter climate: like all the other emirates, it hopes to widen its economic base by encouraging tourism, capitalising on its comprehensive range of high-class facilities and uniquely individual attributes.

Dr Sultan bin Mohammed al Qasimi, author of the treatise exploding the misconceptions surrounding Arab piracy in the Gulf, is Ruler of Sharjah. This relatively small but extremely impressive emirate with a population around 70,000, extends along fifteen kilometres of Arabian Gulf coastline and has a maximum breadth of, approximately eighty kilometres. Situated immediately to the north of Dubai, both emirates share the onshore Margham oil-field. Sharjah, somewhat unusually, also includes territory on the eastern coast, adjacent to the Gulf of Oman, including Kalba, Khor Fakkan, Khor Kalba and part of the ancient and historic town of Dibba, which is also controlled by Fujairah. Sharjah city, capital of the emirate, lies 13 kms north of Dubai. In fact these two cities were linked as recently as 1967 by the region's first asphalt road. Today the country is criss-crossed by manicured, perfectly surfaced dual carriageways. This emirate, site of the town of Mleiha which flourished in the Hellenistic period on a trade route at the foot of the mountains, was also reasonably prosperous in the 1950's, before the discovery of oil had stimulated the economies of the other emirates. The first modern airport was built here and the first modern school in 1953, compounding Sharjah's reputation for intellectual and cultural strengths. But the silting of the creek forcing most of the sea-faring trade further south to Dubai, heralded a decline in Sharjah's fortunes. Oil was discovered in 1974, bringing renewed prosperity but the Saja'a oil and gas field, brought on stream in 1982, has resulted in a great upsurge in development.

In addition to health education and housing development projects designed, as in the other emirates, to guarantee a healthy and comfortable lifestyle for its all of citizens whilst providing them with the education necessary to secure their future, Sharjah has capitalised on its cultural strengths and built a new Cultural Centre, including a large library, theatre, art gallery and other facilities. Sharjah, headquarters of the UAE Arts Society, hosts a very successful Book Fair and its National Theatre Company has recently received an award for a play performed at an Arabian Theatre Festival in Tunisia. Sharjah is also known for a number of elegant and innovative buidings, including some architecturally superb souks. The main sea-port Mina Khalid, is augmented by the strategically valuable port of Khor Fakkan. The latter, sacked by the Portuguese in 1506, has seen rapid expansion in recent years.

Sharjah, served by an excellent international airport, has a broad range of attractions for visitors over and above its innate charm. East coast resorts with many high class hotels will aid considerably in the drive by the Emirates to encourage tourism.

Unlike the other emirates within the Federation, Fujairah does not possess coastline on the Arabian Gulf, but has land stretching along ninety kilometres of the eastern seaboard, bordering the Gulf of Oman. Fujairah is ruled by Sheikh Mohammed bin Hamad al Sharqi who has success-

The UAE is now famous for its efforts at embellishing an otherwise harsh landscape by cultivation projects. Nowhere is this more apparent than at its roundabouts, such as this one in Sharjah, where the nation's dependence upon oil is reflected in a flaming torch. (Vine).

fully grappled with the emirate's developmental problems over a period of time, carefully encouraging projects based upon sound use of local resources. For many years it was the odd man out within the UAE, with no oil and apparently few exploitable features except for a modest fishing industry and limited agricultural potential, although its territory encompases the plain of Al Batinah, one of the most fertile regions in the entire country. In addition, it was for a long time cut off from the rest of the UAE, since the road through the Hajar mountains was frequently impassable as a result of flash-floods. This changed with the completion of an all weather highway in the mid 1970's and, since then, several other important developments have taken place including the opening of an international airport, the establishment of a cement plant, a rock-wool factory, marble and ceramic works, and the expansion of harbour facilities, especially at the port of Fujairah. This latter development has meant the increase in importance of Fujairah as a staging post for ships entering the Arabian Gulf. Although it is situated outside the Gulf, it is strategically placed to pick up cargoes for Gulf countries and for trading with India, Pakistan and Oman. This advantageous location coupled with road improvements means that Fujairah is set to become a main line port with corresponding feeder services. Better road communications have also been of considerable benefit to the traditional agricultural and fishery sectors.

Today, the future for Fujairah seems brighter than ever before in the area of commercial development, whilst its great natural beauty guarded by numerous forts and watch-towers; interesting archaeological remains as at the ancient and scenic city of Dibba, and the Iron Age tomb of Qidfa; stretches of white sandy beaches cradled by rugged mountains; and a rich sense of tradition render it a fascinating and pleasant place to visit, both for residents from other parts of the UAE, and for international tourists in search of something still unspoilt and unique.

Ras Al-Khaimah, with a population around 116,000, is squeezed onto the northern tip of the peninsula, occupying sixty four kilometres of Arabian Gulf coastline just south of the Straits of Hormuz. Encompassing an area of 1,684 sq.kms, and bordering with Oman's rugged mountains, Ras Al Khaimah, unlike the other emirates facing the Arabian Gulf, possesses a narrow coastal plain backed by soaring mountains which, at its most northern point, close to Sha'am village, plunge almost vertically into the sea. A narrow plain between sea and mountains is fed by a useful supply of run-off water and is remarkably fertile, rendering the emirate an important agricultural region. The Ruler, Sheikh Saqr bin Mohammed al Qasimi, has guided the emirate's development from a state of total dependence upon local agriculture and fishing to that of the most recent of the oil - revenue stimulated economies. But despite the new 10,000 barrel-a-day Saleh oil field, emphasis is still placed upon the long-term importance of farming to the emirate's future. The city of Ras Al Khaimah, situated close to the once immensely prosperous medieval Islamic port of Julfar, has grown in the space of a few years from a rather picturesque old-world coastal town to a gleaming modern city. This rapid development is epitomised in the contrast between the old and new sections of the city. However, Ras Al Khaimah's rich heritage has not been abandoned and the opening of a new museum, housed in a picturesque old fort, is an important step in the direction of preservation. Grave goods found in the excavation of the numerous 2nd. millenium tombs and extensive settlement at Shimal join the archaeological and ethnographical material on display in this museum.

With an economy based on natural resources, including agriculture, fishing, rock quarrying and oil, Ras Al Khaimah may have grown at a slower pace than its southern neighbours, but it is blessed with a diversified economic base helping to ensure long-term stability. To the above revenue -earning pursuits RAK, as it is affectionately known, has recently added tourism. It promises to be a field for rapid expansion in the coming years, since the country is one of the most scenically attractive in the Emirates and offers tourists interesting and unusual vacations. Those intrepid visitors who attempt the steep climb to the impressive tumbledown ruins with the romantic name of Sheba's Palace, in reality a medieval Islamic hill fort above Shimal in Ras al Khaimah, will not only be rewarded by interesting ruins but can savour breathtaking views of mountain, desert and sea, the like of which would be hard to equal throughout Arabia, let alone the UAE!

Ajman, covering 259 sq kms and twenty-six kilometres of coastline, is situated between Sharjah and Umm Al Quwain; its landward border comprised entirely of Sharjah. The main part of Ajman consists primarily of the town and land surrounding the port immediately north of Sharjah, but there are, in addition, two small enclaves in the Hajar mountains: Masfit and Manama. Ajman ruled by Sheikh Humaid bin Rashid al Nuaimi, has a strong maritime tradition and the local dhow building yard, the largest in the Emirates, continues to operate despite being dwarfed by modern developments such as the major dockyard. Despite the absence of oil discoveries within Ajman, the emirate has continued to develop its infrastructure and to broaden its economic base.

Despite its small size, Ajman has achieved considerable progress in local development and the provision of services to its citizens; and has carried out an impressive beautification programme, including the establishment and maintenance of two city parks, landscaping of grounds adjacent to main roads and some particularly well manicured roundabouts. Urban development has also been well- planned, employing interesting architectural features in attractive new buildings.

Umm Al Quwain, adjacent to Ajman, on the shores of the Arabian Gulf, possesses slightly less coastline than Ajman, but a larger land area, occupying a total of 777 sq. kms. At its broadest point, it reaches thirty two kilometres inland, incorporating an important and productive agricultural belt at Falaj Al Mu'ala, south- east of the city. Trade with the Mediterranean, northern Arabia, Mesopotamia, and Persia through Ad Dour near Umm Al Quwain in the Hellenistic period spawned one of the biggest cities in all of Arabia now lost forever amongst the sand dunes. But in its recent development, Umm Al Quwain has not forgotten the important place maritime activities

Fishing boats tied up at Ras Al Khaimah's quayside retain the traditional lines of the Arab dhow, while depending upon large diesel engines rather than sails for their power. (Vine)

have played in its past. A new fishing harbour and extensive port facilities have been completed, emphasising the importance of this sector to the local economy. As with other emirates, infra-structure has been greatly improved and Umm Al Quwain is well placed to take further advantage of its natural resources. Recreational facilities include a wide range of sports complexes, horse and camel tracks, as well as a cultural centre and excellent hotels.

The modern miracle of the Emirates' development has been achieved since the British relinquished their colonial control on the country, and the Emirates themselves banded together under the capable leadership of Sheikh Zayed, Ruler of Abu Dhabi and President of the UAE, together with his brother members of the Supreme Council, Rulers of the other six emirates. Despite the difficulties faced by the country during recent years, when oil prices destabilised, the UAE has maintained much of the impetus of its developmental thrust while carefully consolidating gains made in the boom period.

AGRICULTURE

Progress in agriculture during the last decade has been extremely impressive, with government help in the form of loans, technical assistance, and the establishment of demonstration units playing a vital role in the process. As recently as thirty years ago the only visible form of agriculture in the UAE was pastoral, focusing on traditional livestock such as camels, goats and sheep, together with a few scattered date palm plantations. Today there are in excess of four million date palms under active cultivation in the Emirates.

To farmers grappling with the realities of the region's arid climate, its low and irregular rainfall coupled with dessicating winds and searing summer temperatures, the idea of achieving national self- sufficiency in fruit and vegetables, or of developing a broadly diversified agricultural base, seemed nothing more than wishful thinking! Indeed, apart from the uncompromising climate, there were other difficulties to face. Light textured soils were easily eroded and poor in nitrogen, phosphorous and other vital nutrients. In many cases soils had unacceptably high salinity levels and this situation was tending to deteriorate. The Hajar mountain range was however a source of alluvial soils, washed onto the gravel plains along the foot of the mountains by occasional flash-floods. These did provide a relatively suitable medium for agricultural activities, as long as other essential ingredients were added.

In many cases the vital missing element was, of course, adequate supplies of water, not simply in terms of quantity, but also of good quality. A single acre of farm land in the Emirates uses as much as 6,800 gallons per day, and in a country without permanent rivers or lakes, this places a huge strain on resources, with virtually all supplies drawn from subterranean aquifers. Over seventy percent of the Emirates' total water supply is used in agriculture and this has caused a significant drop in the water-table. In some areas salt-water seepage has accelerated, causing further problems. Despite these apparently insurmountable difficulties a policy of water conservation through construction of dams, efficient piping, and modern irrigation methods, coupled with innovative farming techniques especially adapted to local conditions, has brought the country to the verge of self-sufficiency in many food products and made it a net exporter of some items.

National agricultural policy is formulated by the UAE Ministry of Agriculture and Fisheries, headquartered in Abu Dhabi, with regional offices in each of the Emirates. Major agricultural areas are Digdada (Ras Al Khaimah); Falaj al-Mualla (Umm al Quwain); Daid (Sharjah); Fujairah; Al Awir (Dubai) together with the oases at Al Ain and Liwa. For administrative purposes the agricultural areas are split into five regions; the North, comprising Shaam to Hamraniyah; the Central Region, including Dhaid, Falaj al-Mualla, Mleiha, and Masfut; the East, covering Dibba to Kalba; the South, encompassing the Al Ain region and finally the West where Liwa oasis is situated.

Farmers are encouraged to develop their units by attractive financial and technical incentives, including loans for machinery, fertilizers, agricultural equipment, seeds, plants and fencing. New farms can obtain free surveys, fencing, levelling, ploughing, digging of wells and free water pumps. At the same time agricultural advisers insist that farmers comply with crop rotation policies. In order to provide on-site advice and assistance there are forty one agricultural extension units in the UAE, fourteen of which are situated in Al Ain. Efforts are proceeding on a continuous basis and one could point to numerous examples of the beneficial effects of this coordinated agricultural policy. A project launched in Dubai, for example, distributed hundreds of machines for improving irrigation methods and for spraying pesticides, leading to a massive increase in the use of sprinklers, bubblers and drip irrigation systems. The number of farms in the UAE rose from 7,759 in 1977 to 13,590 in 1984 with a proportional rise in cultivated area from 15,339 hectares to 31,751 hectares.

Liwa and Medinat Zayed, in the western region,

supply more than 39 tons of vegetables per day, including 20 tons of tomatoes. At Al Oaha, Al Ain, over 11,000 dunums of wheat were grown in 1986, while production is set to increase further. Although the total cultivable land in the UAE is between sixty and seventy thousand hectares, most of the farms are small, around two to three hectares. Larger projects are mainly concerned with dairy production, poultry farming and cereal crops. Farmers are now encouraged to grow non-traditional crops such as potatoes, cauliflowers, onions, and peas, items which were previously avoided since they are relatively slow growing and less profitable. Smaller farmers still depend on fodder crops for their basic income, with Lucerne taking pride of place, since it can provide up to fourteen cuttings per year, and yield 14.5 metric tons per dunum (fresh-weight). It is also beneficial to the soil, increasing its nitrogen content.

A cornerstone of the country's agricultural development has been the establishment of experimental farms and agricultural research stations at Al Ain, Al Dhaid, Hamraniya, Kalba and Sadiyat Island. The station at Hamraniya (Ras Al Khaimah) for example introduced new melon seeds and investigated virus infections on previous melon harvests while conducting tests in plastic covered houses. Similar experiments were carried out on potatoes, corn, cabbage, aubergine, cauliflowers and hot-peppers. Work on melons by the Central Agricultural Zone has involved the cultivation of sixty one different seed types leading to several very impressive results. A 250 sq.metre greenhouse project established with Japanese government assistance at Al Ain has also aroused considerable interest. The greenhouses are covered with opaque plastic and inside large fans blow a fine water vapour over the crops, cooling and irrigating simultaneously. Crops are grown in a layered combination of peat-moss and sand; or else in a fibrous material manufactured from crushed rock, known as rock-wool.

Success in vegetable production has even led to the establishment of a vegetable canning plant at Abu Samra, 40kms west of Al Ain. This followed a local over-production of tomatoes and consequent dumping of produce. The new factory produces tomato ketchup, tomato juice and tomato puree as well as canning or cling-wrapping fresh cucumbers, carrots and onions. An agricultural survey by FAO identified the northern Emirate of Ras Al-Khaimah as possessing one of the best micro- climates for production of winter tomatoes and this has led to Swiss investment in 'Blend-Fine Emirates' which cultivates a 135 hectare site at Hamraniya and exports hundreds of tons of tomatoes, aubergines, beans, maize and melons annually to Switzerland. The farm management have demonstrated that production in the UAE is more economical than in Europe, where they claim one kilogram of winter tomatoes, grown by modern methods, requires the consumption of three litres of fuel, as well as incurring expensive labour costs. At the time of writing, Ras Al Khaimah is providing sixty-eight percent of the entire UAE's vegetable output and is equally active in other fields such as dairy farming with, for example, the Digdaga Dairy farm maintaining eight hundred milking cows and making a significant contribution to the UAE's 37,000 tonnes annual milk production.

New projects include an abbatoir in Dubai; a fifteen hectare nursery in Sharjah; a new nursery for Dubai Municipality's Horticulture Section at Al Garhood; a 3-5 hectare greenhouse project at Fujairah; a date processing plant at Digdada producing 14,000 tonnes of dates per year (and in the process recycling crushed date-stones as animal fodder); and a feed mill in Sharjah, turning out about 60,000 tonnes of concentrates annually.

Today, the UAE produces dates, citrus fruits, mangoes, guavas, figs, tomatoes, celery, potatoes, carrots, beans, marrows, cucumbers, lettuce, cabbage, melons; peppers; fodder crops; aubergines; at least 8,000 tonnes of eggs and 17,000 tonnes of meat per year. General farm output rose from 192,000 tonnes in 1977 to 712,000 tonnes in 1986.

The great success achieved by the UAE in the agricultural sector has given it a leading role in the Arab World in this field. The UAE has proved, both to its own people and to others, just what can be achieved in even the harshest conditions, providing efficient systems are adopted. In the process, the climate of the Emirates has been marginally altered and the foundations have been laid for continual growth of agriculture in the future.

FORESTRY

The Emirates have placed considerable emphasis upon their "greening of the desert" policy and on the establishment of parks, gardens, tree-lined highways and landscaped roundabouts. Each year the UAE holds a Tree Day, an important event in the calendar widely celebrated by all citizens from government ministers to boy scouts. Thousands of trees and shrubs are distributed free of charge to schools, government offices, institutions and local residents. Saplings are planted along highways and the populace is urged to respect the afforestation programme.

On Tree Day in 1986 Abu Dhabi distributed 20,000 trees to various municipalities and 50,000 shrubs to the general public. In Dibba 1,500 saplings were planted in a single main street while in Khor Fakkan water pumps irrigated 5,500 trees donated to schools and other private residences. All emirates planted vast numbers of trees and shrubs and the effect of this policy can readily be seen in the ever increasing amount of greenery apparent as one drives through the UAE. The trees themselves act as wind-breaks, helping to combat the encroachment of shifting sands.

Throughout the UAE thousands of hectares of land are gradually being covered by greenery. Afforestation companies are regularly awarded contracts for 200 to 300 hectare land-plots. Appointed companies prepare the land, plant saplings over an 18 month period, and then maintain them for two years after which the local forestry department takes charge. Payments are linked to the number of healthy trees at the time of take-over.

The major oases of the UAE, such as Al Ain, are also expanding their afforestation programmes. Al Ain now has forty public gardens, sixty green roundabouts, seven nurseries and hundreds of hectares of trees. Liwa has also been active in this field and trees are provided free to landowners, in order for them to be planted as wind breaks. Similar schemes have been established at Medina Zayed and Al Kharima and an extensive wind-break of trees has been planted along the entire 55kms section of the Bida Zayed to Liwa road. This latter project involved levelling sand-dunes over a width of 225 metres and then filling the strip with massive quantities of top-soil before planting over a thousand hectares of trees.

Drip or trickle irrigation is used in nearly all afforestation projects within the Emirates. Water is pumped from a maximum of 1,000 feet, and distributed via drip lines, arranged in parallel rows, approximately seven metres apart. Two hundred seedlings are planted per hectare, each plant consuming five gallons of water per day for the first year, doubling after that with date palms requiring as much as two to three times as much water as the average arid zone tree. The main trees planted are Samar (*Acacia tortilis*), Ghat (*P.scicigera*), Qarat (*A.arabica*), Sidr (*Z.spina-christi*), and Eucalyptus.

FISHERIES

Prior to its discovery of oil the Emirates turned to the sea as a source of wealth, engaging in pearl shell diving, fishing, and traditional merchant marine activities. Today there are approximately eight thousand fishermen in the UAE (including expatriate Asians), with over three thousand fishing boats, and an annual yield of about 73,000 tonnes of fish, a proportion of which is dried for animal feed and fertiliser. Government policy, as with the agricultural sector, has been aimed at encouraging planned development of fishing through the provision of various financial and technical incentives. All fishermen are eligible for a fifty percent subsidy towards their boats, winches, fish traps, engines, nets and other equipment. In addition the Ministry of Agriculture and Fisheries has established seventeen marine workshops along the UAE coastline, offering free repair and maintenance services. Cooperatives have been formed to assist fishermen in marketing their catch and in obtaining better terms on equipment purchases. In addition training in new methods is provided. An exclusive, twenty-five kilometre wide fishing zone exists around the UAE coastline, effectively preserving inshore fish stocks for locals.

Capital intensive projects have included construction of new fishing harbours and development of a National Mariculture Centre at Umm Al Quwain: a project established in cooperation with the Japanese. Their efforts are concentrated on rearing prawns, tilapia, rabbitfish, mullet and grouper, with all fish fed on pellets manufactured at the centre from locally produced fishmeal. The centre is still in an early phase of development but results to date have been encouraging with 18 tonnes of fish and shrimp reared on an experimental basis in 1986.

Traditional dhow lines are still a feature of the majority of fishing boats, although fibreglass vessels are making inroads into this picture. Virtually all the craft are motorised and the largest vessel or **amlah** can carry up to 40 people. Other craft, such as the **baggarah** and **shu'ai** carry less people but are used for fishing trips lasting several days. Along the coast of Fujairah one may still see that most traditional of fishing boats, the **shashah**, constructed from date palms with the modern addition of polystyrene floats. Most of the fishing boats are locally built, and range in size from about six to twenty five metres in length.

The main equipment in use comprises shrimp trawls, metal wire fish-traps, fishing lines; beach seines; small purse seines; and gill-nets. Fishing activity, tending to concentrate on the winter months, results in plentiful catches which are distributed locally and exported. Demersal (bottom feeding) fish include around forty five marketable species and are brought ashore at any of the UAE's forty landing centres. The major families include groupers, snappers, sea-breams, emperors, threadfin bream, rabbitfish, goatfish and grunts. Among the pelagics, sardines constitute the bulk of the catch, together with their predators including tuna, mackerel, and jacks. Shellfish include the shrimp *Penaeus semisulcatus*, slipper lobster (*Scyl-*

larides sp.) and coral crayfish, *Panulirus versicolor*, crabs (Portunidae), and molluscs.

Sardines and anchovies, caught in vast quantities, are often laid out to dry and then used as animal feed or fertiliser. In 1986, 28,000 tonnes were utilised in this way. For some time local supplies of fresh fish were protected by a ban on exports, but this was modified in 1986, providing for up to 18,000 tonnes to be exported each year.

HEALTH CARE

Once again, it is not simply the achievements of the UAE which impress, but the short time-scale in which progress has taken place. During my research for this book I attended a lecture at Al Ain Natural History Society given by a doctor who had helped to build Al Ain's first hospital. Today, during the lifetime of this same person, the UAE possesses some of the most sophisticated health-care centres in the world and operations performed within the country include complex surgery such as heart valve and kidney transplants. As recently as 1971, the vast majority of the emirates had no health service and yet today, every population centre in the country, however small and remote, is covered by the national health service. Concurrent with this development, efforts to prevent illness have been stepped up and programmes for eradication of malaria have met with considerable success.

Faced with the recent worldwide spread of AIDS, the UAE has equipped itself with diagnostic facilities as well as mounting a programme to achieve self-sufficiency in blood and plasma supplies so that today the country has sufficient local donors to meet requirements. Progress in the field of educational and training programmes for nurses and doctors has also received a boost from the establishment of a medical college associated with the national university. As part of its efforts to encourage international cooperation in the medical field, regular seminars are held in the country, bringing experts from all parts of the world.

A sustained programme of hospital and clinic construction throughout the federation has greatly improved health care facilities for UAE residents. Recent developments in this field include completion of the 374 bed Al Wasl hospital in Dubai. This is the federation's first specialist paediatric and maternity centre. Abu Dhabi Emergency Hospital is another recent project which is to replace the city's Central Hospital, opened in 1966. By the end of 1986 there were around 5,000 in-patient beds in Government owned hospitals throughout the UAE together with numerous other facilities linked to particular institutions such as the armed forces. Private medical centres have also blossomed, with many providing specialist services such as the New Medical Centre in Abu Dhabi which can deal with diving accidents suffered by professional or amateur divers and a number of private dental clinics.

EDUCATION

The first modern school was opened in Sharjah in the mid-1950's. Today the United Arab Emirates boasts a fully integrated educational system catering to almost half a million pupils and students.

Education has been a priority of the UAE since its inception. President Sheikh Zayed is acutely aware that while oil may have provided the means whereby the Emirates have been able to launch themselves into the modern age, the federation's real future lies with its people, and especially its youth. A key to this strategy has been the programme to eradicate widespread illiteracy which was a feature of the population when the British departed. Considerable progress has been made since this time and, today, the UAE is on the verge of achieving a completely literate population: a remarkable achievement in less than twenty years. Formal education in schools, colleges and the university has grown at an equally impressive rate. In 1985-86, there were over 250,000 pupils enrolled in State institutions or private schools, including the University. Over 375 State schools were in operation throughout the country, with 10,777 teachers employed. These were augmented by about a hundred and fifty private schools, attended by about 90,000 students, some of which are geared for particular nationalities of expatriates. In addition, several thousand students attend special schools run by the Ministry of Defence, and at least six thousand students attend the Emirates University at Al Ain. Over half of the students at the University, which was opened in 1977, are girls studying the same curriculum as their male counterparts but attending separate lectures. Tuition, books and accomodation are all free, ensuring that those who have the ability are not prevented from achieving their potential. Within the field of Adult Education, the efforts of the UAE Womens Federation in providing literacy classes for women are of considerable significance.

Fifty-five new schools were planned for construction in 1986- 87 while higher educational facilities were also being developed, including the opening of the University's medical faculty. Given the resources available to it and the lack of any previous significant educational programme, the

UAE has achieved wonders in this field and seems set to meet its objectives of creating an informed and well trained population, providing a sound basis for its future growth.

COMMUNICATIONS

Air travel.

International airports at Abu Dhabi, Dubai, Sharjah, Ras Al Khaimah and Fujairah render the UAE one of the best served locations in the world from the viewpoint of aircraft, passenger and cargo handling facilities. To these modern airports, a new one at Al Ain will shortly be added. A healthy level of competition exists between the different airports, each doing its best to attract passenger and freight business. Their joint success has resulted in the UAE having among the highest transit air-traffic in the world. Passenger buildings have been developed to serve the large numbers of people who pass through the UAE. The new terminal at Dubai for example can handle eight and a half million people per year! One of the big attractions for the short-stay visitor is the duty-free shops at the various airports with those of Dubai and Abu Dhabi earning international awards for their excellence together with reputations for providing some of the world's best value to shoppers.

Emirates, the international airline of the UAE, has wasted no time in making its presence felt alongside the giants of civil aviation. Normally, in the fiercely-competitive world of passenger service, newcomers take years to establish theselves, but today there is a smile on the face of **Emirates,** reflecting the splendid achievements of one of the youngest international airlines in the world. Few could have imagined the rate at which **Emirates** would take shape, and grow, following the Dubai Government's announcement early in 1985 that the UAE was to have its own airline. **Emirates** went from the drawing board to reality in the space of a few months, and profits were being counted just nine months after it began operations. The original number of flights were doubled in the first year, and when **Emirates** began its services into Europe, starting excursions to London on July 6th 1987 and flying to Istanbul and Frankfurt from July 31st 1987, its destinations had almost quadrupled in less than two years. H.H. Sheikh Ahmed bin Saeed Al Maktoum, the young and highly active chairman of **Emirates**, has clear intentions for the airline to become established over many more routes, particularly in the Gulf, Asia, and parts of Europe. When **Emirates** was named among the top ten carriers in the world for its business class by the British magazine 'Executive Travel', it was an endorsement of company policies which managing director Maurice Flanagan, previously a senior executive in British Airways, took comfortably in his stride. "We do not go out of our way to win accolades, but we know what passengers want and we have a management that is responsive and flexible enough to give it to them", he commented.

Sea Transport

The United Arab Emirates has important seaports on both its Arabian Gulf and Indian Ocean coastlines. Fujairah and Khor Fakkan have benefited from their geographical position, outside the Straits of Hormuz, and have attracted a great deal of shipping in recent years. Fujairah for example, increased its general cargo handling by 71 percent in 1985; also registering a 53 percent increase in container traffic. Figures for 1986 indicate that the increased traffic rates have been maintained for this port whose operations are aided by considerable expansion of berthing and handling facilities. On the Arabian Gulf coastline the port of Jebel Ali continues to confound the sceptics who once claimed that such a huge man-made port would never be viable. The new Free Trade Zone at Jebel Ali has attracted many internationally based businesses together with some local companies. During its first year of operating the scheme over sixty companies signed agreements to enter the zone, resulting in its immediate expansion. Several large industrial companies use the port, including the aluminium company, DUBAL and associated cable company DUCAB, while locally situated DUGAS has expanded its operations due to development of the onshore Margham gas and condensate field. The Dubai Dry Dock has also undergone a recent upsurge in business, handling eleven million tons deadweight of shipping in 1985 with increases since then. The dock is able to accommodate ultra large (ULCC's) and very large (VLCC's) crude tankers and to effect repairs on them with an efficient turn around speed. Further south, Mina Zayed in Abu Dhabi is also a busy port, handling vast numbers of containers. In addition Mina Khalid in Sharjah, and Mina Saqr in Ras Al Khaimah have developed alongside the local economies and industries which they serve. The port at Sharjah experienced a rapid boost following the new operations of Saja'a onshore gas and condensate field, injecting more funds into the local economy. Ras Al Khaimah's port handles mainly raw quarried stone for construction projects throughout the

Gulf. The port at Umm Al Quwain has also been developed and will help to serve the new aluminium smelter due to commence operations in this Emirate.

While the airports and seaports of the UAE handle movements of cargoes and people, providing the essential life-blood of the economy, there is another form of traffic which has not been forgotten. ETISALAT was established to coordinate and develop the federation's electronic communications network. Construction of the UAE's fourth satellite earth station at Dhaid has enabled it to link-up with ARABSAT, a project utilising its own satellite network for communications between Gulf countries and other members of the Arab Satellite Communications Organisation, ASCO. An additional project, recently completed, is a new sea-cable from the UAE to India. While these projects have national and international significance, ETISALAT has also greatly improved the national telephone, telex system to a state where it is now one of the most modern in the world. The field of good communications, so essential to a country's development, has been well handled in the Emirates, opening up many possibilities for the state and private sectors.

TRADE AND INDUSTRY

While the UAE's international trade remains dominated by export of oil, gas and related products, there has for some time been an awareness that this situation will eventually draw to a close, and that the country must diversify its commercial activities as far as possible. Apart from agriculture which has already been discussed in some depth, there are a number of other successes in this field, with steady expansion of non-oil related ventures. In 1985 this sector reached 14.2 billion Dhs, or approximately a quarter the value of the oil sector.

One of the prime areas of growth, the re-export trade, has been strengthened by the Free Trade Zones at Jebel Ali and Fujairah. The traditional aspect of sea- trading has also received a boost from improved port facilities, with the UAE being used by many companies as a base for trading throughout the region.

The population of the UAE, presently around 1.6 million, is too small by itself to support any major manufacturing industries; the local market is in fact shrinking because of a recent decrease in disposable income. This complication is compounded by the fact that labour is expensive and most raw materials have to be imported from abroad, eating into the competitiveness of the final product. The private sector can only depend on external markets for growth, meeting headlong the challenge of international competition. One venture to have succeeded internationally is the cable manufacturer DUCAB which has exported to most GCC states. The Ras Al Khaimah rock exporting company is another success story with 250,000 tonnes of rock a month being sent to Gulf countries for construction projects.

The new aluminium smelter at Umm Al Quwain is part of a 640 million development project involving the smelter along with a desalination plant, electric power station and other facilities. It is hoped that the smelter will export aluminium to major clients in China and the USA, and will thus complement the existing aluminium smelter company at Jebel Ali, Dubai.

Progress continues, albeit at a slower and more controlled pace. Today there is an acute awareness of the value of full planning prior to project implementation. Thus Sharjah's recent development of the Saja'a gas field has been accompanied by establishment of a liquefaction plant while Ras Al Khaimah has ensured that onshore projects accompany development of the new Saleh field. There are other examples such as Fujairah's replacement of rockwool imports, vital to agriculture, with its own rockwool producing plant. Whilst there remain limits to how much industrial development can achieve in the UAE, there is no doubt that the lessons of recent years will be applied to guide its future growth in this field.

FURTHER READING

From Trucial States to UAE.
F. Heard-Bey.
Longmans. 1981.

The Origins of the United Arab Emirates. A Political and Social History of the Trucial States.
Rosemarie Said Zahlan.
Macmillan Press, London. 1978.

Gazeteer of the Persian Gulf, Oman and Central Arabia.
J.G. Lorimer
Republished by Gregg International Publishers Ltd. and Irish University Press, Shannon, Ireland. 1970.

UAE, An Insight and Guide.
M. Tomkinson.
Micheal Tomkinson Publishing. 1975.

The Myth of Arab Piracy in the Gulf.
Sultan al Qasimi.
Croom Helm. 1986.

Arabian Sands.
Wilfred Thesiger.
Longmans. 1977.

Desert, Marsh and Mountain.
Wilfred Thesiger.
Collins. 1979.

UAE. A MEED Practical Guide,
2nd edition.
Middle East Economic Digest, 1986.

Petroleum Industry in the UAE,
1984 – 1985 – Yearbook.
Arab Information and Public Relations Establishment 1986.

Ras al-Khaimah, Flame in the Desert.
M. Deakin and R. Constable.
Namara Publications, Quartet Books, London. 1976.

Nabati Poetry,
The Oral Poetry of Arabia.
Saad Abdullah Sowayan.
The Arab Gulf States Folklore Centre, Doha-Qatar. 1985.

Oman, a Seafaring Nation,
The Ministry of Information and Culture, The Sultanate of Oman. 1979.

Pearls.
Their origin, treatment and identification.
J. Taburiaux.
NAG Press, Ipswich, Suffolk. 1985.

Arab of the Desert.
H.R.P. Dickson.
George Allen & Unwin,
London. 1949.

Britain and the Persian Gulf.
J.B. Kelly.
Clarendon Press,
Oxford. 1968.

Abu Dhabi: a portrait
John Daniels.
Longmans, 1974.

History of the Arabs.
Philip K. Hitti.
Macmillan Press, London. 1970.

The Persian Gulf.
Sir Arnold Wilson.
Oxford. 1928.

Petroleum and the Economy of the UAE.
Mana Saeed al-Otaiba.
Croom Helm. 1977.

Looking for Dilmun.
Geoffrey Bibby.
Penguin. 1980

Biology of the Arabian Peninsula,
a bibliographic study.
Dr. Mohammed Ataur Rahim,
Saudi Biological Society. 1979.

World Bibliographical Series,
Volume 43: United Arab Emirates.
Frank A. Clements.
Clio Press, Oxford.

Encyclopedia of Islam
edited by HAR Gibb and others.
Brill, Leiden. 1960.

Birds of the Arabian Gulf.
Michael C. Jennings.
Allen and Unwin. 1981.

Arab Seafaring in the Indian Ocean in Ancient and Early Medieval Times.
G.F. Hourani.
Princeton. 1951.

Emirates Archaeological Heritage.
Shirley Kay.
Motivate Publishing. Dubai. 1986.

Archaeology in the United Arab Emirates.
Vols I, II and III. Dept. of Antiquity and Tourism, Al Ain.

Provisional Constitution of the UAE.
Ministry of Information, Abu Dhabi.

Al-Ma'thurat Al-Sha'byyah.
A specialised quarterly review of folklore published by the AGS Folklore Centre in Doha-Qatar.

Publications of the **Emirates Natural History Group,** Abu Dhabi. PO Box 303, Abu Dhabi.

ACKNOWLEDGEMENTS

This book could not have been written without the cooperation and assistance of a great many people living in the UAE. First of all we must thank the Ministry of Information and Culture of the UAE for their advice and assistance during fieldwork. It is a pleasure also to record our gratitude to the local Ministries of Information in each of the Emirates. Throughout the official visits in connection with this book we were received courteously and hospitably. The task of sourcing data for the book was aided by several individuals and organisations and we should like here to mention Ibrahim El-Abed, Director of Emirates News Agency, WAM; and Abdul Rahim Al-Mahmoud, Undersecretary at the Abu Dhabi Cultural Foundation. We must also express sincere thanks to Reem El Mutwalli at the Cultural Foundation who introduced us to the UAE's artistic community and who contributed her own summary of the UAE art movement for publication in this book. On the same subject, we wish to thank the individual artists who so kindly gave permission for their work to appear.

We are most grateful to Sarah Searight for contributing her own account of UAE's past. Shirley Kay has also enhanced this section as well as other parts of the book, by providing some of her excellent colour slides.

The task of summarising knowledge of natural history in the UAE must necessarily draw heavily upon the research work and field observations of many amateur and professional naturalists who have worked within the region. While we have done our best to present a synopsis of already published works, we have also relied upon the goodwill of local natural history groups, such as the UAE Natural History Society, whose members have played a major part in improving our knowledge of local natural history; often highlighting the need for conservation measures to be employed. We know that many of the people involved have either published, or else are in the process of publishing, personal accounts of various aspects of natural history. We are therefore most grateful for their cooperation with this project, and wish them luck with their own more detailed accounts. In particular we should like to thank Linda Coupland who carried out much of the literature research and wrote an early draft on local natural-history; and the photographers who contributed pictures for this section.

We take pleasure in expressing our thanks to the Intercontinental Hotel in Abu Dhabi for welcoming us and indeed to the Abu Dhabi Hotels Corporation for their interest in this project.

INDEX

Abdul Rahim Salem, artist 117, 118
Abu Dhabi Cultural Foundation 117
Abu Dhabi Eastern Bird reserve 70
Abu Dhabi, founding of 20
Abu Dhabi, modern development 142
Abu Dhabi in 1958 141
Agriculture 152
Air travel 156
Ajman 151
Al Ain 144
Al Ain fort 38
Al Nahyan 29
Albuquerque 18
Anglo-Persian Oil Company 38
Art and Artists 116
Art, development of 116

Bani Yas 20, 29
Beaches 61
Bedouin 17
Birds 66–73
Birds, breeding species 72–73
Boat building 92
British political influence 20–21

Camel 32
Camel breeding 82
Camel racing 100
Climate 46
Coastal shallows 60
Coastal vegetation 49
Communications 156
Construction and design 113
Coral reefs and corals 62
Coupland, Linda 40–42

Date palm 55
Date cultivation 32, 85
Desert and semi-desert plants 50–52
Dibba 16
Diving 64
Dubai 145–149
Dubai creek 139
Dubai creek, bird-life 70

Education 155

Fahidi fort, Dubai 34
Falag 15, 24
Falconry 103
Federation 21, 40
Fisheries 154
Fishing 89
Forestry 153
Forts 34
Fujairah, modern development 149–150

Gazelle 41
Geological features 47–49
Golf Club 137
Graves 26

Hafit, Jebel Hafit 24
Handicrafts 95
Hassan Sharif, artist 124, 125
Health care 155
Hellenistic period 16
Hili 12
Hili, iron-age village 25
Hisham Al-Mathloum 133
Horse-racing 103

Ibn Majid 18
Ibrahim Al Sharhan 132
Insects and Arachnids 78
Introduction 12
Islamic influence 16

Jahili fort, Al Ain 22

Khouloud Salih, artist 128, 129

Landscape 43
Lorimer 18

Magan 12, 14
Mahmoud Al Ramahi, artist 130, 131
Mammals 75
Marine mammals 66
Marine-life 59
Modern Emirates 137
Mohamed Abdullah, artist 136
Mohamed Al Qasab, artist 123
Mohamed Khadim, artist 134
Mohamed Mandi, artist 122
Mohamed Yousef, artist 121
Mona Al Khaja, artist 126
Mosques 140
Music, song and dance 111
Mutwalli, Reem El 116

Nasser Abdullah, artist 135
Natural History 41
Nejaht Hassan Makki, artist 127

Obaid Surour, artist 118, 120
Oil industry, development 39
Oil, discovery 38, 39
Oil, discovery & development 20
Oil, first concession 37

Pearl fishing, decline 37
Pearling 20, 25, 86
Persians 16
Piracy, the Myth of 19
Pirate Coast 12
Plant-life 49
Portuguese 18, 19

Qasimi, Dr Sultan Al- 12
Qattara 14
Qawasim 19
Qawr, Wadi 26
Qidfah, grave site 28

Ras Al Khaimah fort 35
Ras Al Khaimah, modern development 150–151
Reem 41
Reptiles 74
Rumalilah 15, 33

Sabkhas 24, 44
Sand-dunes 45
Sea transport 156
Seagrass beds 61
Searight, Sarah 23
Sharjah 149
Sharjah's corniche souk 138
Shimal 18
Social customs 109

The Past 23
Trade and Industry 157
Traditional dress 109
Traditional sports 100
Traditions 81
Trees and shrubs, list 56–59
Tribal affinities 29–30
Trucial States 12

Umm Al Quwain, modern development 151
Umm an Nar 12, 14, 25

Vasco da Gama 18

Wadis, plants 53
Walid Yasin, Dr 25